Sir John Soane's Museum, London

Sir John Soane's Museum London

Tim Knox

Photography by
Derry Moore

MERRELL
LONDON · NEW YORK

This, my first book, I dedicate to my parents.

Tim Knox
October 2008

Contents

THE PLAN AND INTERIOR
OF THE
GROVND FLOOR
OF A
TOWN HOVSE

An Introduction to the Museum

As the construction and arrangement of the honey-comb manifest the instinctive sagacity of its uneducated builder – as the position and formation of the dwelling of the beaver evince a degree of skill and foresight almost rational – as the geometric symmetry of the spider's suspended and outstretched web shews the cunning of its wily weaver – so does the house of the Architect, the gallery of the Painter, and the library of the Author, exhibit some prominent characteristic trait of its respective owner.

So begins the preface of *The Union of Architecture, Sculpture and Painting*, or 'descriptive accounts of the house and galleries of John Soane' by John Britton (1771–1857), published in 1827 as a guide to the architect's burgeoning collections in Lincoln's Inn Fields, as well as a manifesto of his architectural ideas. The book was an impressive production, dedicated to the king, comprising over seventy pages of text, with twenty-three specially commissioned engraved plates depicting the museum and its principal works of art. It had possibly been inspired by Thomas Hope's (1769–1831) lavish folio volume *On Household Furniture and Interior Decoration*, published some twenty years before, illustrating the stylish 'archaeological' interiors and furnishings of Hope's London townhouse in Duchess Street. The presentation copies of Britton's *Union* were distinguished by a hand-coloured aquatint frontispiece (fig. 2) depicting a view looking into the recently completed Monk's Parlour – with a glimpse of Soane's extraordinary Picture Room arrangements above – encrusted with curios, architectural fragments, models and drawings, the perfect abode of an architect-antiquary.

Luckily for us, Soane's amazing house-museum still survives, so we can compare Britton's description with the museum as it is now. Moreover, the *Union* was not the last guidebook to Soane's museum. Soane, like any serious collector, was constantly acquiring new treasures, and Britton's book was soon out of date. Nor was Soane entirely satisfied; the book was a commercial flop, and there were arguments over money and the ownership of the illustrations.

This determined Soane to be author of the next guidebook to his museum himself, but it was only in 1830 that the *Description of the Residence of John Soane, Architect* appeared, its very title suggestive of its principal source of inspiration, Horace Walpole's (1717–1797) *Description of the Villa of Horace Walpole ...*

Fig. 1
Johann Heinrich Muntz
Horace Walpole in the Library at Strawberry Hill,
pen and wash, *c.* 1759, 530 × 380 mm (20⅞ × 15 in.),
private collection
Reproduced from a photograph in Paget Toynbee (ed.),
Strawberry Hill Accounts ... (1927)

Soane was doubtless influenced by Horace Walpole's collections, and Walpole's *Description* of 1784 of his own house at Strawberry Hill served as a model for Soane's guidebooks to Lincoln's Inn Fields.

OPPOSITE
Fig. 2
Penry Williams, engraved by Richard Havell
The Monk's Parlour,
frontispiece to John Britton's *The Union of Architecture, Sculpture and Painting* (1827),
290 × 220 mm (11¼ × 8¾ in.)

This lavish coloured print served as an introduction to Britton's account of Soane's house and collections. The Monk's Parlour had been created by Soane three years before, in 1824, as an atmospheric adjunct to his new Picture Room, which is just visible at the top of the view.

Fig. 3
Longitudinal Section through the Museum & Crypt,
detail of an etching from John Soane,
Description of the Residence of John Soane, Architect
(1835), plate XXV, 270 × 375 mm (10⅝ × 14¾ in.)

Soane lavished great care on the illustrations in the
guidebooks to his house-museum in Lincoln's Inn
Fields, updating them where necessary to show
changes to the crowded displays. This ambitious
plate of 1835 shows the back of the museum, with
the full-height tribune over the sarcophagus of King
Seti I, and the Students' Room on its mezzanine
over the Colonnade.

at Strawberry Hill, written and published by Walpole himself in 1784 (fig. 1). Soane's *Description* was printed at his own expense and made use of only three of Britton's illustrations; a set of new lithographs was commissioned from Charles Haghe (died 1888) that accurately recorded the new arrangements. A second edition of the *Description* appeared in 1832, with a dedication to HRH the Duke of Sussex and two additional plates. Finally, in 1835, a third edition appeared, limited to 150 copies, with yet more illustrations and a largely rewritten text, reflecting the changes to the museum and the large numbers of new acquisitions (fig. 3). Moreover, Soane's tour was supplemented with 'pictorial and poetic remarks' by Mrs Barbara Hofland, a literary admirer, in order to 'render [it] more pleasing and attractive to young minds'. This third edition contained, printed in full, the text of the 1833 Act of Parliament that Soane had had enacted for the preservation of his creation. This, together with his account of various architectural disappointments, two poems to the memory of Mrs Soane, and a description of Soane's recent apotheosis – the presentation of a commemorative gold medal from the 'Architects of England' – made the 1835

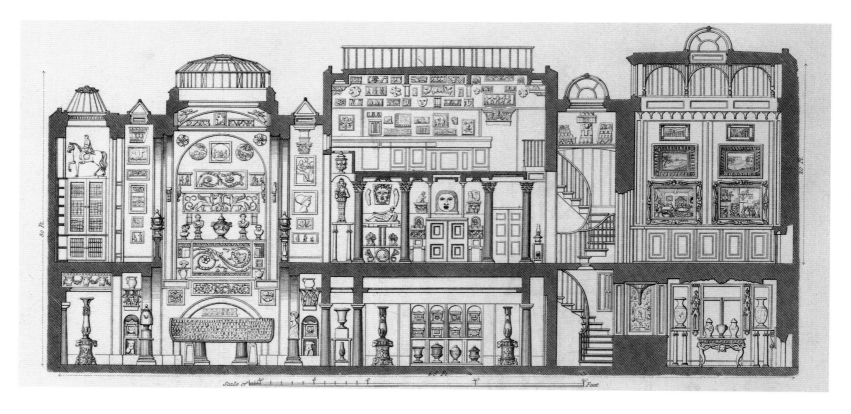

Scale of   Feet

Description very much the testament of the elderly architect, anxious to ensure that his own version was passed down to posterity. Indeed, Soane's 1835 *Description* remains the final word on what his museum should look like, even to this day.

The four guidebooks to Sir John Soane's Museum, together with inventories, letters, sale catalogues, bills and the very accurate watercolours of almost every aspect of his house that Soane commissioned from his pupils, give an extraordinarily complete picture of the evolution of his house-museum. Indeed, perhaps no other historic house collection anywhere is so well and minutely documented. More remarkable is that it almost all survives, thanks to the care with which successive trustees and curators have respected Soane's strict injunction, as set out in his 1833 Act of Parliament: that they 'shall not (except in the case of absolute Necessity) suffer the arrangement[s] … to be altered'. Although after Soane's death the trustees sold some furniture, mainly from the bedrooms, and – maddeningly – threw away such minor personal items as Soane's false teeth and Mrs Soane's knitting needles, the museum survives largely as he knew it – the perfectly preserved house-museum of an early nineteenth-century architect.

The extraordinary accumulations and arrangements of John Soane were hardly typical for an architect-collector of his era. It is true that the Adam brothers (Robert, 1728–1792; James, 1732–1794) and Henry Holland (1745–1806) had both formed collections of drawings and antique fragments, which they displayed in their homes or architectural offices as an advertisement of their virtu and professional status. John Nash (1752–1835) also built himself a magnificent townhouse on Regent Street, with a 21-metre-long (70-foot) gallery, richly gilded and decorated with arabesques after Raphael, containing twenty-two plaster models of celebrated antique structures. Most architects, if they could afford it, formed small working collections of drawings, models and casts to assist them with their designs. Indeed, Soane was to acquire items from the collections of the Adam brothers and Holland, as he was from those of James Playfair (1755–1794), John Sanders (1768–*c.* 1825), Edward Cresy (1792–1858) and Nash. Soane's collecting, however, was altogether more ambitious and wide-ranging. His museum was, in John Britton's words, 'an index, epitome and commentary on the architect's professional abilities'.

Fig. 4
Christopher Hünnemann
Portrait of John Soane, c. 1776, oil on canvas,
590 × 480 mm (23¼ × 18⅞ in.), framed

Hünnemann was a fellow pupil of Soane at the Royal Academy, and this portrait, which is the finest of Soane as an ardent young architect, was probably painted to celebrate Soane's winning the Academy's Gold Medal in 1776.

Born in 1753, the son of a Berkshire bricklayer, Soane was not brought up within a tradition of connoisseurship. A kindly schoolmaster first inspired in him a love of reading, and from 1768, as a clerk in the office of George Dance the Younger (1741–1825), Soane made use of Dance's fine collection of architectural books. As well as being an architect, Dance was also a skilful musician and made sensitive portrait drawings of his friends and contemporaries, so Soane came to appreciate the pleasures and advantages of cultivating the arts. He enrolled in 1771 at the Royal Academy Schools (fig. 4), which had a library and a collection of casts, and in the office of the architect Henry Holland, which he joined in 1772, he would have known his employer's books and ancient marbles. Although Holland's elegantly fitted-up suburban villa, Sloane Place in Knightsbridge, was not built until about 1789, it must have been the model for Soane's later experiment with country life at Pitzhanger Manor; the two men kept in touch long after Soane's return from Italy.

Italy, to which Soane travelled as a young man in 1778 after winning the Royal Academy's King's Travelling Scholarship, must have been a revelation (fig. 5). As well as carefully studying the glorious remains of Classical antiquity, Soane met contemporary Italian architects and antiquaries, including Giovanni Battista Piranesi (1720–1778; fig. 6), and examined the churches and palaces of modern Rome. Visits to private collections, such as an expedition to inspect the curiosity cabinet of the Bishop of Velletri, Stefano Borgia, were a particular interest. Soane travelled to Naples in the retinue of Frederick Augustus Hervey, Bishop of Derry, a rich, omnivorous collector, with whom he saw the excavations at Pompeii and the Royal Museum at Portici. On another excursion, to Sicily in 1779, Soane experienced the nightmarish Villa Palagonia in Bagheria, outside Palermo – often cited as the inspiration for his unconventional use of mirrors – and admired the piled-up arrangements in the museum of the Prince of Biscari at Catania. Back in Rome, there was the famous collection of Graeco-Roman marbles belonging to Cardinal Albani, arranged by J.J. Winckelmann in a sophisticated Neo-classical setting devised by the architect Carlo Marchionni (1702–1786). At this stage Soane was looking and learning, rather than buying – as a struggling young architect on his Grand Tour, early purchases must have been confined to books and prints – although we

Fig. 5
Henry Parke
Royal Academy lecture drawing showing a student on a ladder measuring the capital of the Temple of Jupiter Stator (Castor and Pollux) in Rome, watercolour, 940 × 634 mm (37 × 25 in.)

Soane carefully studied, and often measured, Antique buildings while on his Grand Tour in Italy. This lecture drawing – one of over 1000 such drawings in the museum – was made to illustrate one of Soane's Royal Academy lectures.

Fig. 6
Giovanni Battista Piranesi
*Ancient Intersection of the Via Appia and Via
Ardentina ...*, etching, 395 × 580 mm (15½ × 22⅞ in.),
second frontispiece to *Le Antichità Romane* (1756),
vol. II

This imaginary view of an ancient Roman street of
tombs was typical of Piranesi's exaggerated visions
of the glories of the Eternal City. British Grand
Tourists, and architects in particular, prized
Piranesi's publications as a source of inspiration, and
avidly collected the hybrid confections he conjured
out of Antique marble fragments. Soane befriended
Piranesi in Rome and later amassed a fine collection
of his work.

Fig. 7
Giovanni Battista Piranesi
*Ruins of the Temple of the God Canopus at Hadrian's
Villa, Tivoli*, etching, 445 × 580 mm (17½ × 22⅞ in.),
from *Vedute di Roma* (1748–78)

Soane greatly admired the remains of the villa of
the Emperor Hadrian at Tivoli – now thought to be
the Scenic Triclinium – which he studied during his
Grand Tour of Italy in 1778–80. Ruined vaults, such
as these, inspired Soane's domed top-lit structures.

know he surreptitiously 'liberated' a scrap of Roman painted plaster from the ruins at Pompeii, as a souvenir.

Soane returned to England in 1780, enticed back by the promise of a commission from the Bishop of Derry, who had now also succeeded to the earldom of Bristol. Nothing came of their plans for a palatial country house on the north-west coast of Ireland, however, and for a while Soane struggled to establish himself as an independent architect. Small jobs tided him along – modest country houses, alterations and additions to existing structures, estate and farm buildings – but gave him little opportunity to put into practice the more grandiose architectural ideas he had imbibed during his Grand Tour. Soane's first wholly new-built house was Letton Hall, Norfolk, a large, elegant villa in white brick, comfortable and utilitarian rather than magnificent, in the stripped-down Neo-classical taste he had learned from his masters Dance and Holland. It was begun in 1784, and Soane was still working there eight years later. His attention to detail and his ability to stay within budget recommended him to other landowners, such as Sir Joshua Rowley of Tendring Hall in Suffolk, and Henry Greswold Lewis of Malvern Hall in Warwickshire, where Soane built a witty Doric barn, inspired by the Greek temples he had seen on an expedition to Paestum in southern Italy. At Chillington Hall in Shropshire, Soane retained the ancient walls of the former Great Hall, which he transformed into a spectacular domed saloon lit by an elliptical glazed oculus – a memory of the domed chambers he had seen at Hadrian's Villa in Tivoli (fig. 7). Chillington must have been a welcome challenge for

Fig. 8
Attributed to William Dance
Elizabeth (Eliza) Smith, 1784, miniature,
watercolour on ivory, 41 × 40 mm (1⅝ × 1½ in.)

Soane's marriage to Eliza was a happy one, and her fortune, inherited from her uncle and guardian, George Wyatt, an opulent London building contractor, brought the couple financial security and the funds that enabled them to collect art.

Fig. 9
Antonio van Assen
Mrs Soane with her sons, John and George, c. 1800,
watercolour, 230 × 180 mm (9 × 7 in.), framed

This early watercolour shows Eliza Soane and her two boys, affectionate and docile in their navy-blue skeleton suits. The boys were later to prove a severe disappointment to their parents.

Fig. 10
Joseph Michael Gandy
Aerial cutaway view of the Bank of England from the south-east, 1830, pen and watercolour,
845 × 1400 mm (33¼ × 55⅛ in.), framed

Exhibited at the Royal Academy in 1830 to show the results of Soane's forty-five-year campaign of rebuilding, this ambitious watercolour compares Soane's achievement with the mighty ruins of ancient Rome.

Soane, most of whose work at this stage of his career was depressingly trivial, although it demanded constant attention and a gruelling amount of travel.

In 1784, however, Soane married a young woman called Elizabeth (Eliza) Smith, the niece and heiress of the successful City builder George Wyatt, with whom he had worked while in Dance's office (fig. 8). The new Mrs Soane came with a handsome dowry, and Soane's good fortune was celebrated by the purchase of a house in Welbeck Street, off Cavendish Square, in 1786. Shortly before, Soane had acquired his first articled assistant, one of a succession of pupils who were to pass through his office. Mr and Mrs Soane had two sons, John, born in 1786, and George, who arrived in 1789 (fig. 9). Work continued to come in unabated, including an exotic commission from the exiled William Beckford (1760–1844), for Fonthill Splendens in Wiltshire, where Soane designed a picture gallery lit by a series of domed skylights – a motif that was already becoming something of a Soanean trademark – and a state bed modelled on the Choragic Monument of Lysicrates. Then there were alterations to Holwood in Kent, the villa of William Pitt the Younger, the prime minister. The patronage of the Pitt family was to gain Soane valuable work elsewhere. In 1788 he competed for, and won, the most important job in his whole career, the post of architect to the Bank of England. Over the next forty-five years he was gradually to rebuild almost the entire bank complex, stamping it with his special style (fig. 10).

Old Mr Wyatt died in 1790, leaving virtually all of his fortune and property to Mrs Soane. This, above all, combined with Soane's growing professional success as an architect and his shrewd management of money, gave him the means to indulge to the full his taste for art, architecture and antiquity. Shortly afterwards, the couple purchased a new house, No. 12 Lincoln's Inn Fields, which they rebuilt to Soane's designs, moving there in 1794. The planning of the new house, despite its unusual wedge-shaped site, was conventional enough, but its fitting-up and decoration were distinctively Soanean, with its Entrance Hall and Staircase stippled to resemble sooty masonry, a Pompeiian red Dining Room, and the Breakfast Room, its vault charmingly painted as a fictive convolvulus-hung trellis by John Crace (1754–1819). The charming watercolour by Joseph Michael Gandy (1771–1843) showing the family in their new

Fig. 11
View of the Breakfast Room at No. 12 Lincoln's Inn Fields by Joseph Michael Gandy, 1798, watercolour, 645 × 650 mm (25⅜ × 25⅝ in.)

This rare view of one of the interiors of No. 12 Lincoln's Inn Fields shows Mr and Mrs Soane at table with their two sons. The shrubs visible through the window were arranged in pots on the roof of the Drawing Office Soane maintained at the rear of the house.

Fig. 12
Joseph Michael Gandy
The Bank Stock Office looking north, the Bank of England,
7 June 1798, pen and watercolour, 568 × 941 mm
(22⅜ × 37 in.)

One of Soane's most inventive and austere interiors
at the Bank, a vaulted top-lit banking hall with a
lantern supported on delicate cast-iron ribs. This
celebrated room, destroyed in 1925, has been
re-created in recent years to serve as the Bank
of England Museum.

Fig. 13
Joseph Michael Gandy
The Rotunda, the Bank of England, 1798,
pen and watercolour, 630 × 690 mm (24⅞ × 27¼ in.)

One of the first of Soane's interventions at the
Bank, his Rotunda replaced a lavishly decorated
domed tribune by Sir Robert Taylor, which Soane
demolished on the grounds that it was falling down.
His replacement, which was completed in 1795, was
revolutionary in its simplicity, without columns or
elaborate mouldings.

OPPOSITE
Fig. 14
Joseph Michael Gandy and Antonio van Assen
Lothbury Court looking south, the Bank of England,
1798–99, pen and watercolour, 646 × 952 mm
(25¼ × 37½ in.)

Soane's favourite triumphal-arch motif was
appropriately used in Lothbury Court, a large
courtyard at the back of the Bank site, where bullion
was unloaded and dispatched. The imperial scale of
Soane's Bank of England greatly impressed visitors,
including Alexander I, Emperor of Russia, who was
brought here on his state visit in 1814.

Breakfast Room in 1798 shows a pretty, domestic space, however, with a few Classical prints and plaster statuettes, not the home of a collector (fig. 11).

An important commission came in 1790 from Philip Yorke, 3rd Earl of Hardwicke, who called Soane in to advise on the remodelling of Wimpole Hall in Cambridgeshire. The old house was to be kept, but Soane created an ample trilobe drawing room on the ground floor, with a barrel vault and a soaring top-lit dome. Originally hung with caustic yellow silk, bordered with violet velvet embroidered with arabesques, it was a foretaste of Soane's bold decorative schemes in Lincoln's Inn Fields. For another client, the banker William Praed, from 1793 Soane built Tyringham, Buckinghamshire, a compact bow-fronted house, arranged around a double-height top-lit hall.

Soane's fascination with domed apartments lit from above, with the complex plans of Antique baths and palaces, and with simplified decoration in the most progressive Neo-classical taste, found an outlet at the Bank. There, behind the severe, windowless screen-wall that eventually encompassed the whole site, Soane devised a sequence of large domed banking halls, unencumbered by columns and lit from above – including the Bank Stock Office of 1792, with its simple incised mouldings (fig. 12), and the Rotunda of 1794–95, a spartan pantheon above which floated a lantern supported by a bevy of caryatids (fig. 13). Then there were dramatically treated courtyards and light wells (fig. 14). The Bank was novel, fit for purpose and made daring use of new technology, such as cast iron and hollow bricks.

Fig. 15
Joseph Michael Gandy
The Entrance Front at Pitzhanger Manor, c. 1800,
watercolour, 587 × 915 mm (23⅛ × 36 in.)

Mr and Mrs Soane and the two boys greet visitors
arriving in a carriage. Soane created an imposing
façade for his country villa, garnishing it with
projecting columns surmounted by statues in
imitation of an ancient Roman triumphal arch.
Beyond, the plain wing is what survived of the
original house, a work of 1768 by Soane's old
master George Dance the Younger.

In 1800 the Soanes' income, professional and unearned, was
just over £11,695 – about £350,000 in modern terms. In that year
Pitzhanger Manor in Ealing came on the market, and Soane
bought it for £4500 as a retreat from the noise and dirt of
London. In later life he justified the purchase as 'a house for
myself and family, and afterward for my eldest son, who ... had
also shown a decided passion for ... architecture, which he
wished to pursue as a profession. ... I wished to make Pitzhanger
Manor-house as complete as possible for the future residence of
the young architect.' The object of his hopes was John, then aged
fourteen. The main house at Pitzhanger was rebuilt as a simple
box of white stock brick, with a grandiose frontispiece of four
giant projecting Ionic columns, topped by statues, a motif derived
from Roman triumphal arches (fig. 15). The interior was more
demonstrative, dramatic modelling, lighting and paint effects
being employed to create an atmospheric setting for Soane's
growing collections of antiquities and works of art (fig. 16).

Fig. 16
Joseph Michael Gandy
*Design for the interior of the Library at Pitzhanger
Manor*, 1802, watercolour, 960 × 1295 mm
(37 7/8 × 51 in.), framed

This dramatic watercolour shows the elaboration of
the interiors at Soane's country house, which was,
until its sale in 1810, the principal repository for his
collections. The books in this view play a secondary
role to Soane's collection of Antique Roman
cinerary urns and chests.

Fig. 17
William Owen
Portrait of John Soane, 1804, oil on canvas,
1226 × 980 mm (48 ⅜ × 38 ⅝ in.), framed

Soane, shown with his own, grey, hair, gestures to
an engraving of his favourite Classical structure, the
Temple of Vesta at Tivoli. This circular Corinthian
temple inspired the curved colonnade on the
north-west corner of the Bank of England, a feature
still known as 'Tivoli Corner'.

Fig. 18
William Owen
Portrait of John and George Soane, 1805, oil on canvas,
1226 × 980 mm (48 ⅜ × 38 ⅝ in.), framed

Soane was disappointed that neither of his sons
became an architect, although John, the elder – seen
here with dark hair – did study under Joseph Michael
Gandy. George, the younger boy, was stage-struck
and later quarrelled bitterly with his father.

But it was only at the turn of the century that Soane's 'collectomania' really got going, with a pair of paintings by Canaletto (1697–1768) from the Bute sale in 1796, the Cawdor Vase in 1800, and antique marbles from the 4th Earl of Bessborough's collection in 1801, including a famous statue of the Diana of Ephesus. In 1802 Soane bought more Etruscan vases at James Clark's sale, and a work by Antoine Watteau (1684–1721) from Mr C. Hunter's collection. In that year Mrs Soane bid £570 for William Hogarth's (1697–1764) *A Rake's Progress* from William Beckford's dispersals from his father's Fonthill Splendens. A mummified cat arrived in 1803 (another joined it in 1829), and Mrs Soane bought two watercolours from J.M.W. Turner (1775–1851) in 1804. Soane commissioned portraits of himself and his two sons from William Owen (1769–1825) in that year (figs. 17 and 18), and bought two pictures from the sale of Boydell's Shakespeare Gallery. Pitzhanger as

Fig. 19
Joseph Michael Gandy
Architectural Visions of Early Fancy …,
1820, pencil, pen and watercolour,
735 × 1305 mm (29 × 51⅜ in.), framed

Exhibited at the Royal Academy Exhibition of 1820, this grandiose, palace-strewn landscape was commissioned by Soane as a peevish memoir of all his unexecuted designs for buildings – such structures as a temple-bearing Triumphal Bridge and a grand Neo-classical House of Lords – that were never realized due to official indifference or government parsimony.

Soane envisaged it is best seen in Joseph Michael Gandy's watercolour exhibition perspectives of the house. Gandy, a young architect with a great talent for draughtsmanship, joined Soane's office in 1798. He was to become Soane's favourite architectural draughtsman, a valued and trusted friend, on whom Soane increasingly relied to render his ambitious architectural visions into strikingly dramatic watercolours suitable for display at the annual Royal Academy of Arts exhibitions (fig. 19). Gandy's specially commissioned watercolours were later to become a major component in the displays in Soane's museum.

Most of the important early purchases were displayed at Ealing, which Soane was embellishing in the hope that it would become the seat of the Soanes, a glorious architectural dynasty rivalling the Adams, the Wyatts and Soane's enemies the Smirkes, Robert (1780–1867) and Sydney (1798–1877). In 1808, however, Soane's son John came down from Cambridge without a degree. His health was giving concern. Dispatched to Liverpool to become Gandy's pupil, he was eventually sent back to London, where he contracted an unsuitable marriage. Meanwhile, George Soane was more interested in writing and in the stage. He too married without his parents' permission, and, with his fecklessness, bad temper and predilection for fast company, was soon completely alienated from them.

Soane consoled himself with a new project – another house in Lincoln's Inn Fields. As early as 1807, he was toying with the idea of further extending the house there, purchasing the freehold of the neighbouring house and making plans for an extension behind it to accommodate his plaster casts, many of which had been bought in 1795 from the collection of the Scottish architect James Playfair. Work on the 'Plaister Room' to the rear of No. 13 Lincoln's Inn Fields was under way by 1809, and the structure was complete the following year – the first phase in an unexecuted extension containing galleries for architectural drawings and models, as well as plaster casts and architectural fragments (fig. 21). Soane was by this time Professor of Architecture at the Royal Academy of Arts and wrote of 'arranging the Books, Casts and Models in order that students might have the benefit of easy access to them'. The creation of a quasi-public museum, as opposed to a private architectural Elysium for John Soane junior at Pitzhanger, coincided with a growing realization that neither of his sons would adopt architecture as a profession. In any case, the Clerkship of the Works at the Royal Hospital at Chelsea, a post that Soane obtained in 1807, came with a charming riverside house and garden (fig. 20). So Pitzhanger was sold in 1810, and its accumulated contents moved to Lincoln's Inn Fields. This galvanized the rebuilding of the main house at No. 13; its much larger site gave Soane a building capable of accommodating both his architectural ideas and his collections. The Soanes were installed in their new home by 1813, while No. 12 was let.

Fig. 20
Charles James Richardson
The Clerk of Works' House and Garden at the Royal Hospital, Chelsea, 1833, pencil, pen and watercolour, 236 × 422 mm (10 × 16⅝ in.)

Soane acquired this house in 1807 as one of the perquisites of his position as Clerk of Works to the Royal Hospital. He spent increasing amounts of time there after the death of his wife in 1815.

Fig. 21
Joseph Michael Gandy
*View of the Plaister Room looking south-east
by lamplight*, 1811, pen and watercolour,
1190 × 880 mm (46⅞ × 34⅝ in.)

An atmospheric view of the short-lived precursor
to the Dome area at the rear of the museum.
The space seen here evolved into the Dome, but
many of the casts and antiquities in this view can
be recognized in the museum today.

Fig. 22
Joseph Michael Gandy, *Preliminary design in perspective for the Dulwich Picture Gallery, c.* 1812, pen and watercolour, 740 × 1280 mm
(29⅛ × 50⅜ in.)

This is a design by Soane for the gallery, which was built from 1811, although the need to reduce costs led to the building being simplified during construction. Not only was it the first public picture gallery to be constructed in Britain, but also it incorporated a mausoleum for the donors, enabling Soane to experiment with at least two of his architectural preoccupations: top lighting and commemorative structures. As a building expressly created for the display of works of art, it doubtless inspired his own house-museum in Lincoln's Inn Fields.

Fig. 23
Joseph Michael Gandy
The Plan and Interior of the Ground Floor of a Town House, a collection of views of No. 13 Lincoln's Inn Fields, including the interiors of the Study, the Breakfast Room, two views of the Library and Dining Room, and the Monument Court, 1822, watercolour, 930 × 1500 mm (36⅝ × 59⅛ in.), framed

The rooms carefully recorded in this beautiful composite view are still much the same today, although the painting does not show the mirrors, pictures and other artefacts that Soane added to his collection in the last decade of his life.

Fig. 24
Joseph Michael Gandy
The Soane Family Tomb, April 1816, watercolour, 659 × 972 mm (26 × 38¼ in.), exhibited at the Royal Academy in 1816

The scale of the tomb is exaggerated, and the lush landscape is fictional.

No. 13 Lincoln's Inn Fields is a substantial three-bay house in stock brick, its façade distinguished by a projecting Portland-stone loggia, embellished with incised mouldings and topped by statues. Inside, Soane created an impressive sequence of reception rooms, notably the Library and Dining Room, lined with bookcases and painted his favourite Pompeiian red. Next door was the saucer-domed Breakfast Room, lit from above like one of his counting houses at the Bank (fig. 23). Upstairs, a pair of interconnecting Drawing Rooms, painted a sharp acid yellow, was arranged overlooking the square. But if the creation and decoration of his new house-museum gave him pleasure, Soane himself was not a happy man.

Although Soane's professional successes continued unabated – in 1813 he succeeded James Wyatt (1746–1813) in the coveted position of one of the Attached Architects to the Office of Works, and became Grand Superintendent of the Works to the premier Grand Master's Masonic Lodge – his son George's threatening demands for money had increased, and Soane sternly refused to help, even when George was imprisoned for debt and fraud in 1815. In revenge, on his release George spitefully attacked his father's work in two anonymous articles in *The Champion* magazine. 'He has reared this mausoleum for the enshrinement of his body', wrote George of the house in Lincoln's Inn Fields, while Soane's library was described as 'a satire upon the possessor, who must stand in the midst of these hoarded volumes like a eunuch in a seraglio; the envious … guardian of that which he cannot enjoy'. Soane's mortification can only be imagined. He tried to keep the articles from Eliza, but he recorded what she said when she read them: 'Those are George's doing. He has given me my death blow. I shall never be able to hold up my head again.' Shortly afterwards she retired to her bed, complaining of pains, and died two weeks later. Soane was devastated (fig. 25).

Mrs Soane was buried on 1 December 1815 in St Giles's burial ground at St Pancras. Soane, in deep mourning, framed the articles from *The Champion* and displayed them prominently in his house, inscribed 'Death Blows'. He immersed himself in the design of his wife's tomb, a strange Grecian shrine with a flattened dome, set within its own enclosure (fig. 24). But he kept working – at the Bank, and at the Royal Hospital, Chelsea.

Fig. 25
John Flaxman
Portrait of Elizabeth Soane, 1800–05, pencil,
292 × 228 mm (11½ × 9 in.)

This tender pencil sketch of Eliza was presented to Soane by J.M.W. Turner on the occasion of Soane's knighthood in 1831. Turner had purchased the drawing from the sale of the painter John Jackson, who had used it as a model when painting a posthumous portrait of Mrs Soane in the same year.

Fig. 26
James Ward
Portrait of Fanny, 1824, oil on panel,
240 × 198 mm (9¼ × 7⅞ in.)

This is a posthumous portrait of Mrs Soane's pet
dog, which died in 1820, but is shown here perched
on a capital amidst the ruins of the Erechtheion on
the Athenian Acropolis.

Life went on at Lincoln's Inn Fields, Soane residing there
alone, with only Mrs Soane's terrier, Fanny, for company
(fig. 26). The house was maintained by a staff of five, under the
direction of a housekeeper, Mrs Sarah Conduitt, a family friend,
and of course there were the assistants and pupils in the
Drawing Office. Nor did Mrs Soane's death arrest the continual
stream of objects arriving at Lincoln's Inn Fields: a collection of
twenty-three marbles and sixty-four plaster casts acquired from
the Adam sale in 1818, books and other relics connected with
Napoleon and the imperial family (fig. 27) obtained during a trip
to Paris in 1819, and bronzes from the Cosway collection in 1821.
In 1823 Soane's son John died of consumption. He left a widow
and four young children, to whom Soane remained as stern and
distant as he had been to their father.

More changes were afoot at Lincoln's Inn Fields after Soane
acquired No. 14, the next-door house, which he rebuilt in 1824
as a substantial property to let, annexing its stables to extend
his museum further. In the basement he constructed the
Monk's Parlour, an antiquarian study encrusted with fragments
of medieval ornament, stained glass, and other 'superstitious'
curiosities, illuminated by shafts of golden light from the
yellow-tinted glass in the skylight. Fanny, the dog, which had
died in 1820, was disinterred and buried with great pomp
under a towering monument in a little monastic garden, the
Monk's Yard, outside. Upstairs was the Picture Room. There,
under the elaborate canopied ceiling, hung the series *A Rake's
Progress* by Hogarth, and three Canalettos, supplemented by
a second great Hogarth series, *An Election*, acquired from
Mrs Garrick's sale in 1823. Around them hung a constellation
of smaller works, including a set of bistre drawings of
the ruins at Paestum by Piranesi, and the finest of the Gandy
watercolours. There were, of course, too many pictures,
so Soane devised an ingenious system of hinged 'planes'
on which to display them all. A particularly extravagant
acquisition was the astonishing alabaster sarcophagus of the
Egyptian king Seti I, acquired in 1824 from the late Giovanni
Battista Belzoni (1778–1823); Soane stepped in when the
British Museum refused to produce the £2000 asking price.
The following year he held three splendid parties to celebrate
its arrival, illuminating the house with over one hundred hired
oil lamps.

Fig. 27
The south wall of the Breakfast Room, showing
Napoleonic memorabilia – portraits of Napoleon
Bonaparte (see fig. 120) and a case that once
contained his pistol – hanging beneath a terracotta
relief by John Michael Rysbrack depicting the 1st
Duke of Marlborough receiving the surrender of the
French armies at Blenheim from Maréchal Tallard.

The arrival of the great Egyptian sarcophagus precipitated further changes in the basement at the rear of the house; Soane sacrificed his household offices to create an 'Ante Room' and 'Catacombs' from which to approach the 'Sepulchral Chamber'. Even after the publication of Britton's *The Union of Architecture, Sculpture and Painting* in 1827, the museum was far from complete. Soane's last decade included a series of acquisitions of works by his contemporaries: his portrait by Sir Thomas Lawrence (1769–1830) and a bust by Sir Francis Chantrey (1781–1841) in 1828, *The Passage Point* by Sir Augustus Wall Callcott (1779–1834) in 1829, and Turner's *Admiral Van Tromp's Barge at the Entrance to the Texel, 1645* in 1831. It was almost as if Soane sought to perfect his collections by making them more fully representative: the Adam drawings in 1833 (fig. 28), and, in 1834, a group of gems and illuminated manuscripts bought from the feckless Duke of Buckingham and Chandos; John Flaxman's (1755–1826) original models for sculpture; architectural models from Edward Cresy, and casts from Lewis Wyatt (1777–1853). A late arrival in 1836 was a collection of the drawings by Soane's old master, George Dance, in a monumental cabinet known as 'the shrine'. Anxious, compulsive, buying and building – it is little wonder that Soane's

guidebook, his *Description*, went into three editions in the five years between 1830 and 1835.

The twilight of Soane's career was fully occupied by commissions in and around Whitehall. Commemorated by the Lawrence portrait and the Chantrey bust, Soane had become the Grand Old Man of Architecture (fig. 29). In 1831 he was awarded a knighthood. With one son dead, and the other almost an outlaw, Soane had been planning for some time what to do with his museum. His wishes were crystallized in an Act of Parliament passed in April 1833, by which he vested his house-museum and its contents in nine nominated trustees, who were to open it to the public. Access was to be free; the trustees were not to alter the arrangements in the museum, and Soane specifically desired that amateurs and students of painting, sculpture and architecture were to make use of the collections, which he hoped would become an 'Academy of Architecture'.

Shortly afterwards Soane scaled down his architectural office, retaining only his devoted chief clerk, George Bailey, and an assistant, C.J. Richardson. Improvements continued to be made: the glazing-in of the front loggias, an elaborate new display of architectural models, the addition of more mirrors – probably to bring more light into the house on account of Soane's failing

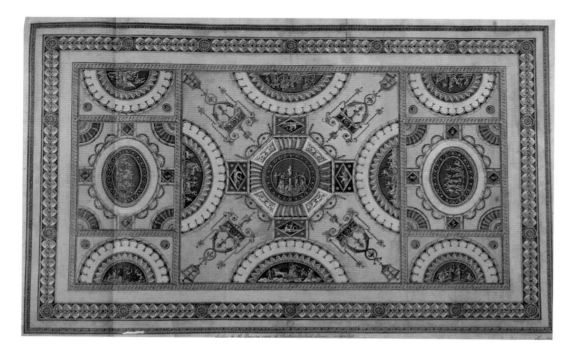

Fig. 28
Robert Adam
Design for the ceiling for the Glass Drawing Room, Northumberland House, London, as executed, 1770, pencil, ink and watercolour, 617 × 982 mm (24⅜ × 38¾ in.)

Soane bought more than 9000 drawings from the office of Robert and James Adam in 1833, paying only £200 for the collection after it failed to sell at an auction in Edinburgh.

Fig. 29
Sir Thomas Lawrence's *Portrait of Sir John Soane*,
1829, oil on canvas, 1390 × 1105 mm
(54¾ × 43½ in.), shown *in situ* over one of the
chimneypieces in the Library-Dining Room

The work shows Soane aged seventy-five, sporting
the alarming auburn wig he wore in later life. It is
one of Lawrence's best male portraits, and Soane's
muse, Mrs Barbara Hofland, claimed it was a
'speaking likeness'.

Fig. 30
Soane's Gold Medal, obverse and reverse,
designed by William Wyon, 1835, gold,
58 mm (2⅜ in.) diameter, 5 mm (¼ in.) deep

Presented to Soane in 1835 by the 'Architects
of England', and silver and bronze copies were
presented to subscribers. The reverse of the
medal bears an image of the Tivoli Corner of
the Bank of England, considered by many to be
Soane's masterpiece.

Fig. 31
View of the Breakfast Room, showing the north wall,
with Flaxman's cast of a statuette of Victory placed
in front of Joseph Michael Gandy's watercolour of
the Soane family tomb. The yellow light comes from
the hidden skylight, a long pitched transom glazed
with primrose-tinted glass.

Fig. 32
Sir Francis Chantrey's marble bust of Sir John
Soane, carved in 1828, mounted on a marble lion's
paw and flanked by John Flaxman's statuettes of
Michelangelo and Raphael. The statuettes were
fixed into this position on Soane's orders, two
weeks after his death.

sight. He also worked on his *Memoirs*, as well as involved
accounts of the iniquities of his son and grandson. On 20 June
1835 he was honoured by the presentation of a gold medal from
the 'Architects of England' (fig. 30). Since he was too frail to
attend the ball held in his honour that night at Freemasons' Hall,
his bust, garlanded with laurel, presided over the festivities.

Soane died on 20 January 1837, from a chill. He was eighty-
three years old. He was arranging his treasures right up until the
end. Ten days before his death, he installed in the Breakfast
Room, in front of a Gandy view of his wife's tomb, a Victory
recently acquired from Flaxman's collection (fig. 31). Soane was
buried, with little ceremony, in the family tomb at St Pancras,
and, after his simple funeral, statuettes of Raphael and
Michelangelo were fixed in the positions he had appointed for
them – at the feet of his own bust by Chantrey, symbolizing
Soane's firm belief in the superiority of architecture over the arts
of painting and sculpture (fig. 32).

Time has been harsh to Soane's built legacy. His works in
Westminster were all destroyed after the fire that swept through
the Houses of Parliament in 1834, and his buildings in Whitehall
were mainly rebuilt in the late nineteenth century. Except for its
outer wall, the Bank of England was demolished in the 1920s.
The Dulwich Picture Gallery (1811–12; fig. 22) was damaged
during World War II, and Soane's Infirmary and other buildings
at the Royal Hospital at Chelsea were destroyed. Of his country
houses, Tyringham has been altered, Tendring Hall has gone,
and Pell Wall has been gutted.

Soane's reputation as an architect also experienced a decline.
Although he had many pupils, none carried on his peculiar
style, and inevitably the next generation found his innovations
mannered and mongrel. The Gothic architects of the Victorian
era deplored his flimsy 'pagan' architecture (fig. 33), and there
were several determined attempts to close the museum down –
not least by Soane's son George and grandson Frederick, who,
disappointed of their inheritance, challenged Soane's will in the
courts. Their suit passed into Chancery and was resolved only
on the abolition of that court in 1873. A more surprising critic
was the architect William Burges (1827–1881), one who might
have appreciated Soane's bizarre, heaped-up arrangements.
'Something should be done about this ... very useless
institution,' Burges complained in 1863, 'an Act of Parliament

Fig. 33
Augustus Welby Northmore Pugin
Contrasts: House Fronts,
engraved plate from *Contrasts …* (1838),
190 × 231 mm (7½ × 9⅛ in.)

Pugin satirizes Soane's house in Lincoln's Inn Fields,
comparing its 'papery' façade with a rich specimen
of medieval domestic architecture.

might surely be obtained for handing over the pictures to the National Gallery, the library and the librarian (salary included) to the Institute of British Architects, the sarcophagus, manuscripts and antique gems to the British Museum … the rest of the collection is of very little value.' By the turn of the century the museum had become notoriously deserted and irrelevant; Henry James made it the unlikely setting for an illicit romantic encounter in his novel *A London Life* (1888). Its limited opening hours – three days a week in only certain months of each year – may have contributed to its air of melancholy abandon (fig. 34).

But, although it was dowdy and unvisited, the museum was preserved largely as Soane knew it. The first curator, the faithful George Bailey, completed a thorough inventory of the contents and published the first *Handbook* about the museum and catalogue of its Library. Bailey and Mrs Conduitt (who acted as the museum's first Inspectress) both died in 1860, and Bailey was succeeded by Joseph Bonomi, an eminent Egyptologist. Less reverential was the energetic and persuasive James Wild, curator from 1878, who erected in 1890 the domed New Picture Room at the rear of No. 12, on the site of Soane's old office and first Picture Room. Wild also rearranged the stained glass throughout the museum, and replaced failing stone floors with cast-iron and glass industrial pavements (fig. 35). His death in 1892 mercifully brought to a halt his ambitious plans for further rebuilding. After a succession of curators – Wyatt Papworth, George Birch and Walter L. Spiers – Arthur T. Bolton took charge in 1917. Bolton is remembered as one of the greatest of all the museum's custodians, and his scholarly publications on Soane and Adam are still classics of their kind.

Oddly enough, it was the outcry at the demolitions at the Bank of England in 1925 that helped to refocus public attention on Soane (fig. 36). Bolton and the trustees of the museum protested vociferously, but at a time when there was no official protection for historic buildings, Soane's masterpiece was largely destroyed. Even if the battle for his bank was lost, Soane's reputation, however, began to be restored. Not only was his contribution to the architecture of the Regency era recognized anew, but he was also even imitated (fig. 37), and the perfectly preserved arrangements of his own residence in Lincoln's Inn Fields came to be revered as a rare, even unique, survival. More recently, architectural historians have found Soane to be a richly

SIR JOHN SOANE'S MUSEUM IN LINCOLN'S-INN-FIELDS: THE SARCOPHAGUS-ROOM.—SEE PAGE 619

Fig. 34
Victorian visitors to the Soane Museum in the Sepulchral Chamber, engraving, 360 × 253 mm (14¼ × 10 in.), from *Illustrated London News*, 25 June 1864, p. 616

The wide, hooped crinolines of Victorian ladies forced nineteenth-century curators to simplify some of Soane's crowded displays.

Fig. 35
An early twentieth-century photograph showing James Wild's extension to the museum, the New Picture Room. New displays, such as this, destroyed Soane's carefully juxtaposed arrangements of artefacts in his museum. Photograph reproduced in A.T. Bolton (ed.), *The Works of Sir John Soane*, Sir John Soane's Museum, 1924, p. 75

documented source of study, while twentieth-century architects admired his simple lines and innovative use of construction and lighting, claiming him as a prophet of both the Modern Movement and Post-Modernism.

During World War II, the museum narrowly escaped destruction by incendiary bombs and much of the glass was blown out of the windows. Some of its more portable contents were evacuated to the country, the sarcophagus remaining in the crypt, protected by a mountain of sandbags. Bolton died in 1945 and the architectural historian John Summerson was appointed in his stead. It was largely through Summerson's efforts that the museum was repaired and reopened in 1947. The museum's own trust funds being utterly exhausted, it was Summerson who persuaded the Treasury to provide an annual grant to ensure that

it remained open – a grant that is still paid to this day and covers about two-thirds of the basic running costs. No. 12 Lincoln's Inn Fields, long let to tenants, was reoccupied by the museum in 1969. Sir John Summerson – he was knighted in 1958 – presided over the museum until 1984, producing a series of magisterial books and articles, including several on Soane (fig. 38). Summerson's successor, Peter Thornton, inherited what was still virtually an Edwardian institution, administered by a staff of three, a manual typewriter and one telephone. Downstairs, it was guarded, with almost feudal deference, by a band of elderly warders. Thornton established a new system of maintaining the records of the works of art and began fund-raising to carry out essential repairs and redecoration. With wide experience of restoring historic interiors, such as those at Osterley Park and

Fig. 36
Frank Yerbury
The Colonial Office of the Bank of England in the course of demolition, c. 1925–26, photograph

Ironically, the destruction of Soane's masterpiece, the Bank of England, raised public awareness of his importance as an architect.

Fig. 37
The K2 telephone box, designed by Sir Giles Gilbert Scott in 1924–26

Scott was a Life Trustee of the Soane museum. The flattened dome of the kiosk, together with its incised linear mouldings, were inspired by Soane's work, especially the Soane family tomb.

Fig. 38
Leonard Rosoman
Portrait of Sir John Summerson, 1984, oil on canvas,
1521 × 1220 mm (59⅞ × 48⅛ in.), National Portrait
Gallery, London (NPG 5730)

Sir John Summerson reigned over the Soane
museum as its curator for forty years, a tall,
commanding presence whose tours every
Saturday afternoon became a London institution.

Ham House, for the Victoria and Albert Museum, Thornton applied his formula of scrupulous research and careful reconstruction to Soane's interiors – sometimes with controversial results, as in the sulphurous Soanean livery of the North and South Drawing Rooms in 1986, or the burnished gilding of the frames of Hogarth's *An Election* in 1987. On his retirement in 1995, Thornton modestly claimed to have left the Soane a 'tidier, cleaner and more colourful museum', but his scholarly brand of showmanship also restored the drama and meaning to Soane's creation. His successor, Margaret Richardson, continued the restoration of the fabric and historic features, and embarked upon more detailed cataloguing of the collections. It was she who established the programme of temporary exhibitions, not only to display hidden treasures from the Library, but also to put on thought-provoking shows with contemporary architects and designers who have been inspired by Soane. In 1996 she acquired No. 14 Lincoln's Inn Fields (which had not formed part of Soane's bequest in 1837), reuniting the Soanean ensemble on the north side of the square. Her successor, Tim Knox, who was appointed in 2005 as the first director of the Soane, oversaw the restoration of Nos 12 and 14 Lincoln's Inn Fields, and inaugurated a further major scheme – still ongoing – to reinstate the historic interiors of all three houses.

Since the mid-1990s, Sir John Soane's Museum, derided and rarely visited in its first hundred years, has undergone a remarkable revival in popularity. It now welcomes more than 100,000 visitors a year – numbers indeed that threaten to overwhelm the fragile interiors and collections. In the last few years the museum has concentrated on repairing the buildings and putting back lost elements of Soane's original displays, as well as cataloguing the myriad collections – many of them, such as the Library, manuscripts and architectural drawings, unseen by the general visitor. The recently completed restoration of the adjacent houses has given the museum much-needed facilities, freeing up more space in No. 13 to reinstate Soane's historic arrangements. In particular, this has allowed for the re-creation of Sir John's modest Bedroom and Bathroom, his diminutive 'Oratory', and his display of architectural models on the second floor of No. 13 Lincoln's Inn Fields, as well as Mrs Soane's Morning Room. Here, in Soane's private rooms, visitors can reflect upon his powerful, but all-too-human, genius.

Fig. 39
Joseph Michael Gandy
Design Perspective for the Front Elevation of 13 Lincoln's Inn Fields, August 1812, watercolour, 780 × 445 mm (30¼ × 17½ in.)

This view shows the projecting Portland-stone loggia with its incised mouldings and Coade-stone caryatids – statues of Grecian maidens. Mrs Soane's Bedchamber and Morning Room lay behind the terrace on which the caryatids stand.

A Tour of the Museum

Today, Soane's three houses on the north side of Lincoln's Inn Fields look like a single, planned composition, but in fact their genesis is much more complicated than that (fig. 40). Indeed, the façade of Sir John Soane's Museum is a good demonstration of its founder's very personal architectural style, and of how his buildings slowly evolved.

Soane's first house in Lincoln's Inn Fields was the left-hand house, No. 12, which was rebuilt by the architect for his own use in 1792–94. Constructed of fine white bricks from Suffolk – now much blackened with London soot – it is an elegant but undemonstrative townhouse, with little ornamentation save the strigillated ironwork of the balcony ('strigillated' is a scrolling pattern named after the ancient Roman *strigil*, a curved spatula used by bathers). Note also the witty string course above the second floor, using bricks laid vertically to imitate the stone triglyphs (literally 'three stones') found in Classical friezes.

But Soane soon outgrew No. 12, and, a few years before the sale of his country villa in Ealing in 1810, he began negotiations to buy the next-door house, which occupied a much larger site, to accommodate all his collections. This was finally achieved in 1812, and the Soanes moved into their new house in 1813. No. 12 was then let, and although it formed part of Soane's bequest of 1837, it was reoccupied by the museum only in 1969. It was restored in 2011–12, and now houses improved visitor facilities: a shop, a gallery for temporary exhibitions, and conservation studios, as well as a discreet lift.

PLATE XV.*

OPPOSITE
Fig. 40
Nos 12–14 Lincoln's Inn Fields – the exterior of the
museum. Looking at the unified façade of the three
Soane houses on the north side of Lincoln's Inn
Fields, few realize that they are the result of three
successive building campaigns: No. 12 in 1792–94,
No. 13 in 1812–13 and No. 14 in 1824.

Fig. 41
*Plan, sections and perspective view of the Recess or
Loggia on the 2nd floor of No. 13 Lincoln's Inn Fields*,
lithograph from Sir John Soane's *Description …*
(1832), plate XV*, 380 × 275 mm (15 × 10⅞ in.)

This plan shows the Loggia as open; Soane later
glazed it in.

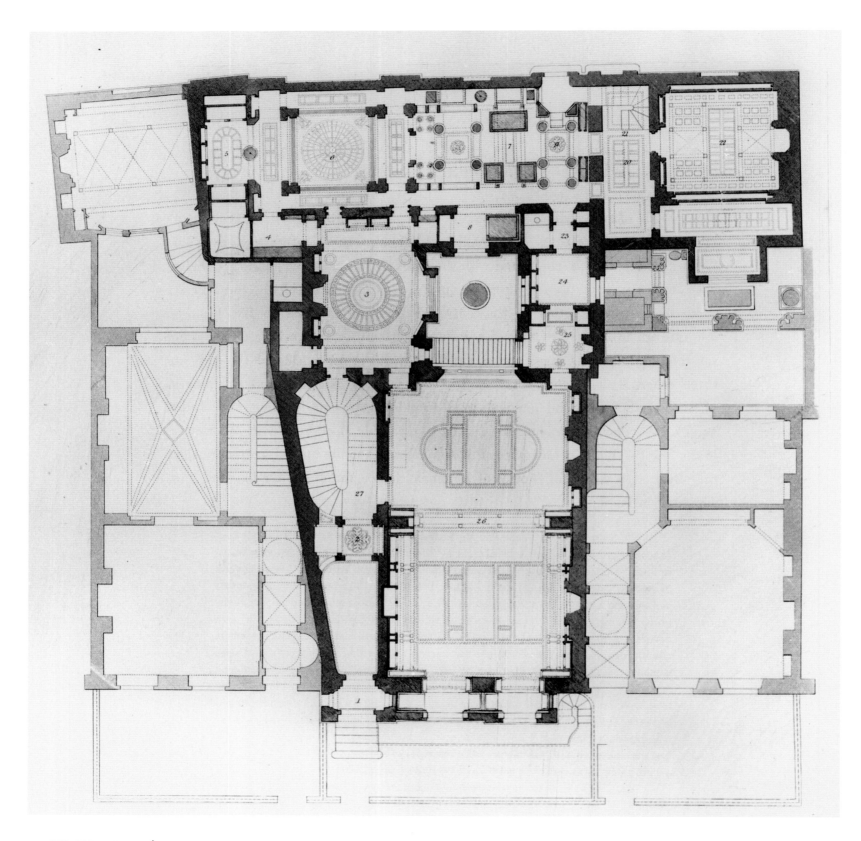

50 SIR JOHN SOANE'S MUSEUM, LONDON

No. 13 Lincoln's Inn Fields was also
built of brick – London stocks – but has
a projecting two-storey loggia in crisply
cut Portland stone. Three bays wide and
articulated with two tiers of arched
openings, surmounted by a little squared-
off belvedere, it is solemn and grand, and
deliberately unlike anything that had been
built before, ancient or modern. All the
apertures on the front were originally open
to the elements; Soane claimed that the
open loggias were 'balconies' – a deliberate
ploy to get round planning regulations.
Even so, his dramatic projecting portico got
him into trouble with the District Surveyor,
who prosecuted him for encroaching
beyond the building line. But the narrow
balconies he created were of limited
practical use and must have made the
rooms inside very dark, so he gradually
glazed them in – the ground floor in 1829,
the first and second floors in 1834. The
narrow 'gallery' Soane devised along the
front of the first-floor Drawing Room
is an example of how he constantly and
inventively embellished his house-museum.
The bringing forward of the windows must,
however, have robbed the façade of some
of its original external drama.

The stonework of the façade is smooth
and simply treated, with incised decoration
around the arcade on the ground floor
and Soane's favourite variation on 'Greek
key' ornament above (fig. 39). He loved
incised ornament and used it everywhere –
especially on the Bank of England –
although critics derided his 'pilasters
scored like loins of pork'. The four strange
projecting brackets are medieval, removed
from Westminster Hall during Soane's
restoration of 1818. Oddly enough, they
never supported statues. Farther up,
perched on the terraces flanking the
belvedere, is a pair of stern, Classically
draped maidens. They are made from
Coade stone, a patent frost-proof artificial
stone manufactured to a secret recipe by
Mrs Eleanor Coade Jr in her factory in
Lambeth. Soane was a good customer

of Mrs Coade, and her architectural
ornaments appear in a number of his
buildings. The statues themselves are based
on the famous caryatids, pillars in the form
of women, that support the porticoes of
the Erechtheion on the Athenian Acropolis.
In decorating his austere façade with Gothic
and Grecian sculpture Soane proclaimed
the museum within to the outside world.

Mrs Soane's private apartments lay
behind the little belvedere and we know
that flowers were grown in pots on its
sunny balconies. Did she sit out here with
Fanny, her dog? Thus the *acroteria*, the little
domed finials decorated with honeysuckle
motifs, and the much-eroded antique
statuette of some animal, are a fitting
garniture for her private eyrie (fig. 40).
More *acroteria* surmount the balustrade that
runs along the parapet of the building, and
Soane articulated the plain brick garrets
of the house with a framework of incised
stone pilasters.

The third house of the ensemble, No. 14
Lincoln's Inn Fields, externally a close copy
of No. 12, was rebuilt by Soane in 1824. He
never occupied this house – it too was let –
but as well as bringing in rent, it gave Soane
a suitably deferential balancing 'wing' to
flank the imposing portico of his house-
museum (fig. 42). No. 14 did not form part
of Soane's bequest to the nation and was
retained by his executors until the 1870s.
It was bought back by the museum, with
the help of the Heritage Lottery Fund and
other donors, in 1996. It was restored in
2006–07 to provide facilities for the
educational programme, the Research
Library and staff offices.

The back of the museum faces a narrow
mews called Whetstone Park – named after
a notorious pleasure garden that once
occupied the site. The windowless façade
is a little-known Soane composition,
economically built of plain yellow stock
brick with a few simple stone dressings.
The projecting pedimented aedicules –
surrounding real and false doors – may owe
something to Newgate Prison, designed by

Fig. 43
Joseph Michael Gandy
The Entrance Hall, c. 1824, watercolour, 221 × 128 mm
(8¾ × 5 in.)

This view shows the Hall as much emptier than
it is today, with only a set of chairs ranged round
the walls.

Fig. 44
Attributed to Joseph Michael Gandy
Detail from *The Inner Hall, c.* 1824, watercolour

The Entrance Hall leads to the Stair compartment,
painted to resemble yellow Siena marble.

Soane's great mentor, George Dance the Younger, in 1769–70. In Soane's day, the westernmost door, now blocked, gave access to the Drawing Office, so that his employees and pupils did not need to pass through the house to get to work.

Sir John Soane's house-museum is entered via a narrow **Entrance Hall**, its dark walls 'coloured to imitate porphyry' (figs. 43 and 44). Above the **Inner Lobby** hovers a fleshy decorative boss, based on an original from the portico of the Temple of Mars Ultor in Rome. In Soane's day, messengers or ordinary visitors waited here on a set of high-backed hall chairs.

The splendid cantilevered **Staircase** makes the most of the irregular site of No. 13 Lincoln's Inn Fields – which is much wider than its façade would lead us to believe – and rises the entire height of the house in a series of leisurely stages (fig. 45). The handsome cast-iron balustrade, with rosettes and a polished mahogany handrail, gives way downstairs to simple ironwork, leading to the kitchens and service rooms in the basement. The walls of the Staircase are skilfully painted to resemble yellow Siena marble. Now beautifully darkened with time, the marbling dates from 1925 and is a replica of the original scheme.

Fig. 45
A glimpse of the lower flight of the Staircase, with James Durno's painting *Falstaff in disguise led out by Mrs Page*, painted for Alderman Boydell's Shakespeare Gallery in Pall Mall and bought by Mrs Soane for 9 guineas in 1805.

To the right lies Soane's **Library and Dining Room**, the largest room in the house; its walls are lined with tall glass-fronted bookcases (fig. 46). Soane was a passionate bibliophile and his library is especially rich in architectural books, although he also collected novels, travel guides, auction catalogues and even cookery books. Highlights include first editions of all four folios of Shakespeare's plays, and what is possibly the baron Dominique-Vivant Denon's (1747–1825) own copy of his *Description de l'Égypte* (1809). Mirrors were used by Soane to bring light into this cavernous room; notice the way he has used them over the chimneypieces and bookcases, on the shutter boxes, set in niches and even in the base of the pier table. Convex mirrors capture the room in their fish-eye lenses, while at night – when Soane liked to entertain here by candlelight – huge sheets of looking-glass can be slid across the windows, making the room resemble a glittering casket.

The room is painted in Soane's preferred Pompeiian red, set off by bronze green (fig. 47). Soane had visited Pompeii in 1779, but the decoration and architecture of the room were also probably inspired by an ancient painted chamber that he had witnessed being excavated earlier that year in the gardens of the Villa Negroni in Rome. Copies of Angelo Campanella's (1746–1811) engravings recording the frescoes in this room are displayed next door in the Breakfast Room (fig. 49). The 'canopy' that divides the two halves of the room looks almost Gothic or Jacobean in inspiration; Soane was extensively employed on works on Westminster Hall in 1819 and 1820. The two white marble chimneypieces are masterpieces of Soane's distinctive stripped-down style, the traditional Classical repertoire of paired pilasters and a frieze being reduced to a series of sleekly carved channels and grooves (fig. 48).

The room is mainly furnished with mahogany pieces, some of them specially

Fig. 46
The chimneypiece wall in the south end of the Library-Dining Room, with Soane's distinctive seat furniture upholstered in wine-coloured leather. Above, 'Etruscan' vases perch on and behind Soane's 'canopies'.

LEFT
Fig. 47
Detail of a pier in the Library-Dining Room. The slender bronzed colonnettes – inspired by structures depicted in ancient Roman murals – frame small bronzes and the 'Englefield Amphora', a finely painted Apulian vessel of the fourth century BC.

ABOVE
Fig. 48
Soane's characteristic incised decoration defines the flanks of the Library-Dining Room chimneypiece.

Fig. 49
Angelo Campanella
*Mural decoration of the Antique Room from the
Villa Negroni, Rome*, 1778, coloured engraving,
560 × 643 mm (22 × 25⅜ in.)

Soane witnessed the excavation of this remarkable
ancient interior during his stay in Rome in 1778,
and the murals were to influence the decoration in
the Library-Dining Room. A set of the prints hangs
in the Breakfast Room.

made to Soane's designs, although the spectacular set of Chinese chairs is made of *padouk*, an oriental rosewood, and was ordered by Sir Gregory Page of Wricklemarsh, Blackheath, whose arms, inlaid with mother-of-pearl, are borne on each chair (fig. 50). Also of note is the astronomical clock by Raingo of Paris, its orrery supported by a circular Classical temple, which Soane bought from the Duke of York's sale in 1827 for £75. He paid £68. 5s. for the large Apulian krater (or wine-mixing vessel) at the north end of the room, the largest and finest of the many 'Etruscan' vases (as they are always known, though in fact they are Greek colonial wares) that perch on brackets and bookcases around the room. It was found near Lecce in southern Italy in 1790 and is known as the Cawdor Vase, after a former owner. The ceiling of the Library and Dining Room is decorated with inset canvases by Henry Howard (1769–1847), commissioned by Soane in 1834. Those over the dining table represent the story of Pandora and her casket, 'whence ... issued all the cares and miseries of life'; Mrs Soane is supposedly the model for the figure of Night in a black veil. Soane's portrait by Sir Thomas Lawrence shows him at the age of seventy-five, and is one of the artist's masterpieces. Opposite is a 'fancy' picture by Sir Joshua Reynolds (1723–1792) called *Love and Beauty*. Both are surrounded with mirrors, so that they look as if they are suspended in mid-air (figs. 50 and 51).

Fig. 50
Mirrors – over doors, behind bookcases and pictures, and in thin strips on the piers that divide the room – break up the planes of the Library-Dining Room in a bewildering profusion of reflections.

Fig. 51
Sir Thomas Lawrence's portrait of Soane from
1829 presides over the north end of the Library-
Dining Room. The carpets are a close copy of the
originals, supplied by the Axminster manufactory
in 1823 for £81. 15s.

OPPOSITE
Fig. 52
The Cawdor Vase, an ancient Apulian wine-mixing
vessel of the late fourth century BC, is silhouetted
against the great north window of the Library-
Dining Room. Beyond emerges the top of
the *Pasticcio*, the architectural centrepiece
of the Monument Court.

Soane used this top-lit room (see right and opposite) as a **Study**, writing letters on the little kneehole desk with a pull-out table that fits neatly under the window. Daylight was controlled by 'dwarf Venetian blinds' in the windows, while the room was kept warm by a fireplace – its jambs made up from ancient marble fragments – and a central heating system that forced hot air up through the circular pierced grilles in the floor. The walls, and even the ceiling, are encrusted with marble fragments of ancient Roman architectural decoration, part of a collection purchased in Rome in 1794–96 by the architect Charles Heathcote Tatham (1772–1842) for Soane's old master Henry Holland. The array of marble lions' paws (the feet of Graeco-Roman tripods or thrones) displayed around the window is complemented by a giant sponge, a natural creation of strikingly paw-like form. Soane enjoyed arranging his treasures in such thought-provoking juxtapositions. A lantern filled with yellow glass, in primrose and amber tints, bathes the ensemble with golden light (figs. 53–55).

Figs. 53, 54 and 55
Sir John Soane's Study is an intimate space, its walls
and shelves crowded with ancient Roman marbles –
fragments of Antique decoration. Yellow glass
in the skylight overhead ensures that these are
bathed in a golden Mediterranean light – Soane's
'*lumière mystérieuse*'.

Next door is a tiny oak-grained **Dressing Room**, which Soane utilized to smarten himself up for meetings with clients (fig. 56). The pump, the washbasin and its casing were re-created in 1990 from the evidence shown in a view in the 1835 edition of the *Description of the Residence of John Soane, Architect*. The ceiling, with its skylight above – one of Soane's most elaborate – incorporates an architectural model for a dome for Freemasons' Hall, and the walls are hung with Soane's early drawings and other memorabilia, including his design for a Canine Residence, created in Rome in 1778 for the son of the Bishop of Derry.

To the east can be seen the **Monk's Yard**, with its 'ruins' constructed of genuine thirteenth-century stonework salvaged from the Old Palace of Westminster. On the other side is the **Monument Court**, once again decorated with architectural fragments. Its central feature is the *Pasticcio*, a preposterous eight-storey totem pole of piled-up architectural features erected by Soane to show the progress of architecture. A finial in his special style surmounts this strange compilation (figs. 57 and 58).

Fig. 56
The Dressing Room provided facilities for Soane to wash and smarten himself up before meeting clients in the nearby Library-Dining Room. Small architectural models and portraits of lady friends jostle for attention beneath the elaborate ceiling and lantern.

Figs. 57 and 58
The Monument Court in the heart of the museum is dominated by the *Pasticcio*. It was re-erected in 2004, incorporating original and new elements – including a Moorish capital from the royal tomb complex at Marrakesh, Morocco.

A narrow doorway leads into a columned gallery filled with casts of sculpture and architectural ornaments. The wooden cupboards under the **Colonnade** (fig. 59) once housed fifty-four volumes of drawings by Robert and James Adam, acquired by Soane in 1833, now kept in the museum's Research Library in No. 14 Lincoln's Inn Fields. Here are some important antique marbles (figs. 60 and 61), notably a draped female torso, a fragment from the frieze of the Erechtheion at Athens, and Soane's celebrated statue of the Ephesian Diana, a miniature copy of the famous idol denounced by St Paul. The body, carved with curious animals and serried ranks of 'breasts' (supposedly bull's testicles or votive purses), is ancient, and was once in the collections of Pope Julius III and Cardinal Pio, but it has been much restored since. Soane bought it from the Earl of Bessborough's sale in 1801.

Fig. 59
The Colonnade at the rear of the museum is lined with an enfilade of wooden Corinthian columns. They support a mezzanine, used by Soane's assistants as a drawing office, and shelter Graeco-Roman marbles.

PICTURE ROOM

Figs. 60 and 61
The marmoreal denizens of the Colonnade include
a miniature copy of the celebrated cult statue of
Diana of Ephesus (opposite) and this snarling
Roman fountain mask (right).

Figs. 62 and 63
More residents of the Colonnade: (left) John
Flaxman's plaster model for his memorial statue
to William Pitt the Younger – a work executed for
the City of Glasgow in 1808–09 – and (opposite)
a plaster statue of Hercules Hesperides, which was
once owned by Flaxman.

Figs. 64 and 65
A plaster head of the goddess Diana, 'from the original found at Bath', sits on a press (opposite), while an antique version of the Venus of Cnidos occupies one of the recesses (right).

The wooden Corinthian columns forming the Colonnade – themselves possibly salvaged from the Bank of England – support a top-lit mezzanine that Soane used as his **Students' Room**. In Soane's day up to six of his pupils worked here at two long drawing benches, surrounded by architectural casts from which to draw inspiration. This, an architect's drawing office of the Regency era, is a unique survival, although for structural reasons it can be visited by only a very few people at a time, by special appointment (figs. 66–69).

The **Museum Corridor** serves as an anteroom to the Picture Room; both were added in 1824 when Soane bought the next-door house and annexed its back yard to provide more room to display his collections (figs. 70–74). The Corridor had its distinctive floor reinstated in 2005, with metal grilles illuminating the basement below. Once again, the skylights are fitted with yellow glass; Soane thought that golden light, or as he termed it '*lumière mystérieuse*', improved the appearance of the plaster casts. In the days before photography or extensive foreign travel, plaster casts were the most accurate way of reproducing architectural details and were thus essential aids to study. Soane's collection, built up over the years by purchase and gift, is extremely comprehensive, and encompasses Classical, Gothic and even Egyptian motifs.

Figs. 66 and 67
A simple wooden staircase (opposite) curls up from
the Museum Corridor to Soane's Students' Room
on the mezzanine. Here (above), inaccessible to the
general visitor, lies a perfectly preserved early
nineteenth-century architect's drawing office, its
walls and ceiling crowded with architectural casts
and models.

PREVIOUS PAGES
Fig. 68
The Students' Room looking north, showing
the extensive collection of casts of Classical
architectural ornament.

Fig. 69
Soane's pupils and assistants worked at long
wooden counters in the mezzanine Students' Room,
surrounded by a reference collection of casts. This
view, looking south-west, shows how light filters in
from the long skylights.

Fig. 70
The Museum Corridor serves as an anteroom to the Picture Room, and as a setting for yet more plaster casts. Full-size casts of part of the cornice and a capital from the Temple of Castor and Pollux at Rome hover over arrangements of Antique marble fragments.

Fig. 71
The Museum Corridor: scrolling consoles frame
casts above the door to the Picture Room.

Fig. 72
The Museum Corridor: casts, a convex mirror and
the base of a Roman fountain.

Fig. 73
Roman fragments: a relief depicting a chariot, and
a marmoreal willow tree.

Fig. 74
The original model for Thomas Banks's monument
to Penelope Boothby. When exhibited at the Royal
Academy in 1783, it moved Queen Charlotte to tears.

Soane's **Picture Room** is lit by an elaborate canopied skylight, its curious hybrid style – half Classical, half Gothic – being one that Soane favoured in the 1820s and 1830s (figs. 75–77). With its elaborate marble chimneypiece, brass shelf and mahogany presses inlaid with ebony, Soane spared no expense in providing a splendid setting for his pictures. He was also inordinately proud of the ingenious hinged panels, or 'moveable planes', that open to display yet more pictures. By this arrangement, Soane wrote in his *Description* of 1835,

The small space of 13ft 8in. in length, 12ft 4in. in breadth, and 19ft 6in. in height … is rendered capable of containing as many pictures as a gallery of the same height, 20ft broad and 45ft long. Another advantage to this arrangement is that the pictures may be seen under different angles of vision.

The lower parts of the room are painted the original shade of drab olive green, a sombre foil for the bright gilding of the picture frames.

In 2011 the Picture Room was rehung to reproduce exactly the arrangement of pictures as it was in January 1837, at the time of Soane's death. Thus, Canaletto's *View of the Riva degli Schiavoni, Venice* (fig. 78) now hangs over the chimneypiece, surrounded by gouache views by Charles-Louis Clérisseau (1721–1820). Soane doubtless intended the Canaletto

Figs. 75 and 76
Left, top: Charles James Richardson, *The Picture Room, c.* 1830, watercolour, 203 × 154 mm (8 × 6 in.), showing Soane's Indian furniture arranged in the centre of the room. Sadly, the filigree ivory table and four 'burgomeister' chairs (left) are too fragile to be displayed there now.

OPPOSITE
Fig. 77
The east wall of the Picture Room has been rehung to its exact arrangement on Soane's death in 1837. Canaletto's magnificent view of Venice (see also fig. 78) hangs above Soane's curious chimneypiece, a hybrid of Classical and Gothic motifs.

Fig. 78
Antonio Canaletto
Detail of *View of the Riva degli Schiavoni, Venice*, 1736,
oil on canvas

One of the most beautiful and impressive of all
Canaletto's Venetian views; Soane bought it from
William Beckford's sale at Fonthill Splendens in 1807.

Fig. 79
The north wall of the Picture Room with the planes
open, revealing *The Passage Point* by Sir Augustus
Wall Callcott (top) and, below it, the eight scenes of
A Rake's Progress by William Hogarth.

Fig. 80
A distracted scullion pours a cask of brandy into
a half-barrel of filthy slops. Detail from William
Hogarth's *An Election, Scene I, An Election
Entertainment*, 1744–45, oil on canvas.

to appear as if it were a window overlooking the Venetian lagoon. Two more Canalettos hang above it, flanking a watercolour by Richard Westall (1765–1836) depicting Milton composing *Paradise Lost*. The north and south walls display the famous set of four pictures by Hogarth entitled *An Election* (figs. 80–81). Painted in 1754–55, at the very height of the artist's powers, they served as models for a popular series of satirical engravings. They once belonged to the celebrated actor-manager David Garrick, who probably commissioned their superb gilded Rococo frames. Soane bought them for 1650 guineas at the sale of the effects of Garrick's widow in 1823. Two views of India by William Hodges (1744–1797) hang above them on the north side, while an atmospheric set of drawings of the Greek temples at Paestum by Piranesi face them on the south wall.

The planes on the north wall open to reveal the eight pictures of *A Rake's Progress*, painted by Hogarth in 1733–34, and acquired by Soane in 1802 at the sale of the great collector William Beckford (fig. 79). These famous pictures were also the basis for a celebrated set of engravings, published in 1735, which tell the moralizing story of Tom Rakewell, a young man who comes into a fortune but dissipates it by an excess of drink, gaming and women, ending his days in Bedlam, still tended by Sarah, his faithful childhood sweetheart. If it is a surprise to encounter such well-known pictures hidden away behind the planes, remember that in Soane's day these pictures were considered rather vicious, and the story of Tom must have reminded Soane only too forcibly of the variegated career of his youngest son, George. The pictures of *A Rake's Progress* are shown in the same order in which Soane displayed them – doubtless to enable him to relate their story more effectively to visitors – while above them is *The Passage Point*, a luminous imaginary view of an Italian lake by Sir Augustus Wall Callcott.

Fig. 81
William Hogarth
An Election IV, Scene IV, Chairing the Member,
1754–55, oil on canvas, 1015 × 1270 mm
(40 × 50 in.), framed

The victorious Tory candidate is paraded through
the streets by an unruly mob. Note the fleeing
swine, including the swimming piglet escaping
across the open sewer.

Fig. 82
Joseph Michael Gandy
*Public and Private Buildings Executed by Sir John
Soane between 1780 and 1815*, 1818, pencil, pen and
watercolour, 725 × 1293 mm (28⅝ × 50⅝ in.), framed

This work was exhibited at the Royal Academy in
1818 and shows more than one hundred of Soane's
executed buildings arranged in a fictional Soanean
chamber, illuminated by the glare of a lamp.
The draughtsman in the foreground may be
Soane himself.

Fig. 83
Joseph Mallord William Turner
St Hugues Denouncing Vengeance on the Shepherd of Cormayer in the Valley of D'Aoust, 1803, watercolour, 676 × 1060 mm (26⅝ × 41¾ in.), framed

One of three works by J.M.W. Turner in Soane's collection, this atmospheric watercolour of a spectacular mountain scene must have reminded Soane of his own journeys over the Alps in 1778 and 1780.

The south planes in the Picture Room are the most impressive, opening to reveal a broadside of elaborate watercolours celebrating Soane's own architectural triumphs, all painted by his talented protégé Joseph Michael Gandy (fig. 82). But, in a further theatrical flourish, the planes open up a second time upon the **Picture Room Recess**, a capacious top-lit light well, crammed with yet more pictures and sculpture. In the centre stands a statue, Sir Richard Westmacott's (1775–1856) original plaster model for his now-destroyed statue *Nymph unclasping her Zone* (fig. 84); below is an architectural model for the south front of the Bank of England, a commission that Soane called 'the pride and boast of my life' (figs. 85 and 86). The pictures include a *fête champêtre* by Watteau, more works by Gandy, and Turner's *St Hugues Denouncing Vengeance on the Shepherd of Cormayer*, a dramatic mountain landscape (fig. 83). Many of Soane's pictures were purchased from his contemporaries at the Royal Academy of Arts.

Fig. 84
A glimpse into the Picture Room Recess through a glass panel in the Museum Corridor, revealing a Roman bronze cauldron, a portrait of the actor John Philip Kemble as Coriolanus by Sir Francis Bourgeois, and Sir Richard Westmacott's statue *Nymph unclasping her Zone*.

Figs. 85 and 86
The Picture Room with its planes half open to
reveal the Picture Room Recess. The architectural
model at the feet of the statue of the Nymph is
Soane's design for the south front of the Bank of
England. Golden light filters down from a lantern
glazed with yellow glass.

Figs. 87 and 88
The Monk's Parlour, created by Soane in 1824 as an
atmospheric setting for his collections of medieval
casts and curios. The *Madonna and Child with Saints*
over the chimneypiece is a reduced copy of an
altarpiece by Fra Bartolommeo in the cathedral
at Besançon. The windows, and even the internal
doors, of the Parlour are filled with old painted
or coloured glass.

Figs. 89 and 90
Detail of the Monk's Parlour chimneypiece, and
a cast of medieval carved foliage.

Aug 22. 1825

View of the Court of the Monk's Grave, looking Eastward on Fidel's Monument.

Fig. 91
Joseph Michael Gandy, *View of the Court of the Monk's Grave ...*, 22 August 1825, watercolour, 262 × 208 mm (10⅜ × 8¼ in.)

A view of the Monk's Yard looking east. Mrs Soane's pet dog Fanny is in the imposing monument, constructed out of architectural salvage.

Fig. 92
The Monk's Yard looking towards Fanny's tomb today, after a comprehensive restoration in 2005.

Downstairs, passing the **Monk's Cell** with its gilded altarpiece and an anatomist's skeleton that once belonged to Flaxman, the visitor enters the **Monk's Parlour**, an atmospheric antiquarian study decorated with Gothic curiosities, including many casts of medieval ornament (figs. 87–90). Inspired by the monastic ruins he had seen on a tour of the north of England in 1816, and doubtless by accounts of Sir Walter Scott's (1771–1832) picturesque arrangements at Abbotsford, Soane created these rooms – and the **Monk's Yard** visible outside through the stained-glass windows – with a rare display of humour. In his *Description*, he tells us that this is the 'Parloir of Padre Giovanni', a fictitious solitary monk, who is buried, with his faithful dog, beneath the monument in the yard outside (figs. 91 and 92). 'Padre Giovanni' is, of course, the *alter ego* of the lonely widower, John Soane himself, and the dog – Mrs Soane's Manchester terrier Fanny – really was interred inside the elaborate monument in the Monk's Yard, which is reverently inscribed 'Alas Poor Fanny'. Bottle tops and bottoms – evidence of Soane's unmonastic taste for fine champagne – can be seen embedded in the pebble pavement of the Monk's Yard.

Fig. 93
The Egyptian Crypt is reached by a simple staircase. The grille – which forms part of the floor of the Museum Corridor – allows light dimly to illuminate the gloom of the sepulchral labyrinth Soane created in his former wine cellars.

OPPOSITE
Fig. 94
A life mask of Sarah Siddons, *c.* 1800, plaster on wooden board, 215 × 164 × 125 mm (8⅜ × 6⅜ × 5 in.)

Siddons was an actress famous for her tragic roles.

Fig. 95
Charles James Richardson, *The Egyptian Crypt*, 1836,
watercolour, 214 × 272 mm (8⅜ × 10¾ in.)

This view shows the compartments containing
models and monuments, as well as the lost
pavement composed of pebbles and champagne
bottle tops and bottoms.

View in the Crypt. 1836 (looking North East.)

Fig. 96
View of the Basement Ante Room, lithograph
from the 1835 *Description* of Soane's museum,
270 × 370 mm (10⅝ × 14⅝ in.), plate XIX

This room is gradually being returned to its
appearance in this view.

Fig. 97
View in the Catacombs, lithograph from the 1835
Description of Soane's museum, 270 × 380 mm
(10⅝ × 15 in.), plate XX

This view shows the Catacombs as they appeared
on Soane's death, an arrangement that will
eventually be reinstated.

OPPOSITE
Fig. 98
Charles James Richardson
View of part of the Collection of Antiquities …,
9 September 1825, watercolour, 389 × 223 mm
(15⅜ × 8¾ in.)

A view of the Sepulchral Chamber and the
sarcophagus of Seti I. Soane celebrated the arrival
of the sarcophagus with three parties in 1825,
illuminating the interior of the coffin with lamps.

The basement of the galleries Soane built at the rear of his house provided him with a dark and atmospheric space in which to display items, many of them of a lugubrious character (fig. 94), from his collections. Thus, a former wine cellar was pressed into service as the **Egyptian Crypt** (fig. 93), with niches containing cork models of Etruscan sepulchres, funerary sculpture by Flaxman and Chantrey, and a copy of the epitaph from Mrs Soane's tomb (fig. 95). The **Basement Ante Room** had displays of busts (fig. 96), while the *loculi* of the top-lit **Catacombs** contained antique Roman *cippi*, or marble chests for the ashes of the dead (fig. 97). The Crypt was kept deliberately gloomy, relieved by occasional dramatic shafts of light through the grilles above, except for the large **Sepulchral Chamber** (figs. 98 and 100) under the light-filled Dome. Here Soane installed the famous ancient Egyptian sarcophagus of King Seti I, which he purchased in 1824 for £2000 after it was rejected by the trustees of the British Museum as being too expensive (figs. 101, 102 and 103). It was perhaps Soane's most celebrated acquisition. The sarcophagus, carved from a single monolith of semi-transparent aragonite and covered with incised hieroglyphs, dates from about 1279 BC, and is one of the most spectacular Egyptian antiquities outside Egypt. Around it are ranged busts, vases and other relics, including the lid of an Egyptian mummy case. The large bronze bust of Pluto was given to Soane in 1833. Its setting, a 'triumphal arch' composed of architectural fragments and a mirror, was reinstated in 2011. Another arch, to the east of the sarcophagus, will be put back in due course, as will other lost features in the Crypt.

Sept. 2. 1825.
View of part of the Collection of Antiquities — from the head of the Seros. —

Fig. 99
Objects in the West Corridor include the *Head of Nepthis* (top left), a cast of an Egyptian coffin-lid fragment, and a seventeenth-century English bust (bottom left) said to be of John James Heidegger, 'master of the revels to King George II'.

RIGHT
Fig. 100
View of the brightly lit Sepulchral Chamber from the gloom of the Crypt.

Figs. 101, 102 and 103
The sarcophagus of Seti I, Egyptian, *c.* 1279 BC,
alabaster, 2775 × 1117 × 813 mm
(9 ft 3 in. × 3 ft 8 in. × 2 ft 8 in.)

Mounted on two ancient fluted columns, probably
from Hadrian's Villa at Tivoli, the sarcophagus is
carved from a monolith of aragonite, a stone
commonly called Egyptian alabaster. These views
show the coffin after recent conservation cleaning,
without the nineteenth-century glass case that
usually protects it.

OPPOSITE
The image of Goddess Nut, guardian of the soul of
the dead king, is incised into the floor of his coffin.

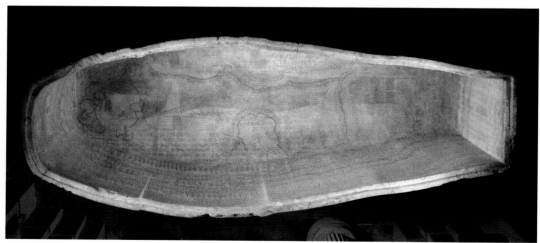

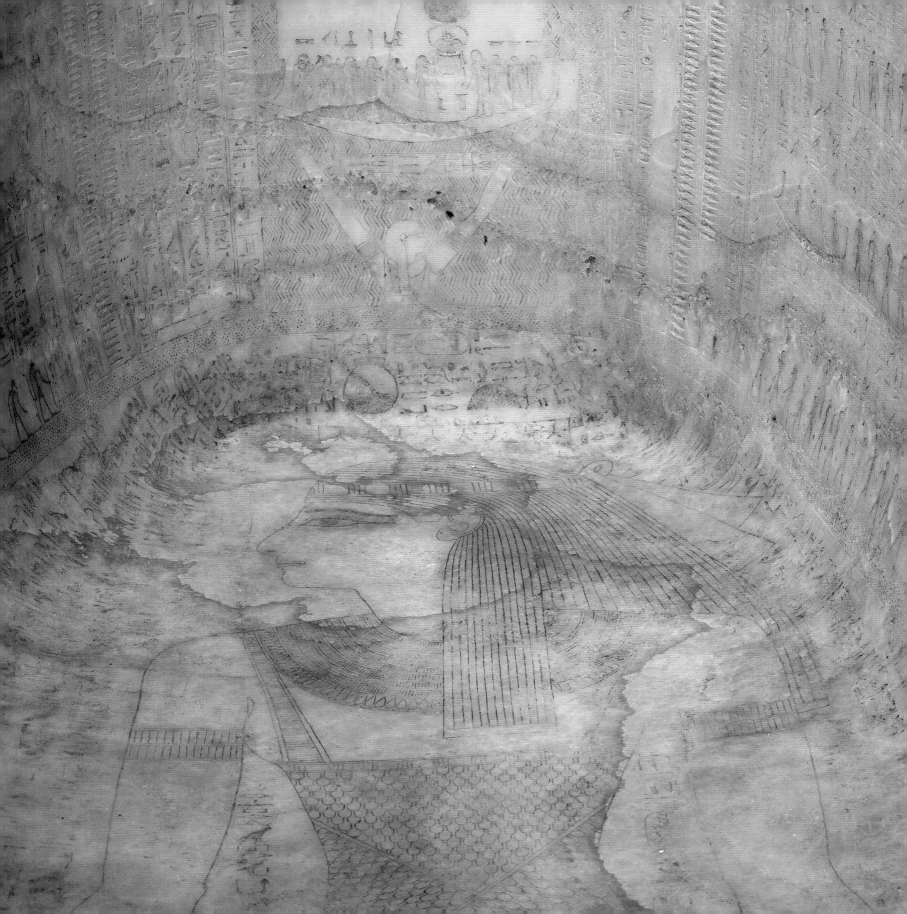

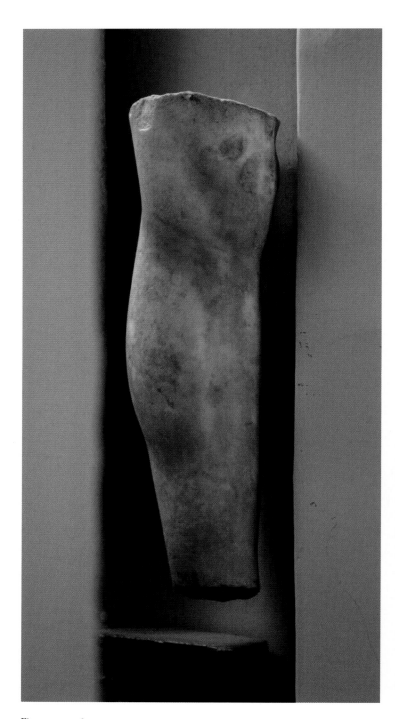

Figs. 104 and 105
A Graeco-Roman limb, said to have been found in
the Circus of Caracalla, Rome, in 1819 and presented
to Soane by Sir Francis Chantrey, is displayed in
the Crypt, and an Imperial second-century bust of
a bearded youth can be seen on the north side
of the sarcophagus.

Fig. 106
A Roman bust of a young man silhouetted against the light-filled Sepulchral Chamber.

Fig. 107
Vista looking west through the South Passage, with a cast of a bull's head.

Fig. 108
A plaster cast of William Sievier's bust of Sir Thomas Lawrence surveys the Dome area.

Looking up from the Sepulchral Chamber, the visitor gazes at the **Dome**, the central light well where Soane created a full-height tribune to display his choicest antiquities (figs. 108–15). Here, under a conical glass skylight, tier upon tier of busts, reliefs and other antiquities rise up, many perching on projecting brackets attached to the balustrade, others fastened to the piers of the arches. The light from the Dome is cunningly supplemented by additional skylights, some of them glazed with yellow glass, prompting Soane's friend the poetess Barbara Hofland to comment on 'that exquisite distribution of light and colour which, often from undiscovered sources, sheds the most exquisite hues, and produces the most magical effects, throughout the Museum, thereby communicating the only charm in which an assembly of marbles must be deficient'.

Many of the exhibits are actually plaster casts, for Soane happily mixed genuine marbles with plaster copies, valuing the assembly above all as a reference collection of models for architectural ornament. Presiding over the company is Soane's own bust by Sir Francis Chantrey, mounted on a giant marble lion's paw. Opposite stands a full-size cast of the *Apollo Belvedere* (fig. 117).

Figs. 109 and 110
The Dome, with Sir Francis Chantrey's bust of Sir John Soane surrounded by cinerary urns and sculptural fragments.

Figs. 111 and 112
The Dome

OPPOSITE
A Roman bust of an elaborately coiffed woman
catches a beam of sunlight.

RIGHT
The north wall of the Dome with its stratified
arrangement of casts of Antique friezes.

Figs. 113, 114 and 115
Details of sculptural fragments in the Dome area.

Fig. 116
Soane's pupils worked in a cramped
mezzanine Drawing Office, behind the bust
of Sir Thomas Lawrence.

OPPOSITE
Fig. 117
The Apollo Recess (off the Dome) looking north,
with a plaster cast of the *Apollo Belvedere*. This
statue was once the property of the famous 3rd,
or 'architect', Earl of Burlington, and was given
to Soane in 1811.

In Soane's lifetime, the statue of Apollo
was seen against a backdrop of mirrored
bookcases, but in 1890 the museum was
extended by the addition of the New
Picture Room, a lofty domed room, built on
the site of Soane's Drawing Office at the
back of No. 12 Lincoln's Inn Fields. The
mirrored recess has now been reinstated,
and the room has been renamed the **Foyle
Space**, a venue for small temporary
exhibitions and a place for visitors to rest
and learn more about the museum and its
collections. It will also be used to display
hidden treasures from Soane's collection,
such as the bejewelled hat badge worn by
Charles I at the Battle of Naseby in 1645,
and a mummy's head.

To the south of the Dome, visitors enter
the **Ante Room**, a narrow, corridor-like
lobby lit with a long, half-round skylight
filled with yellow glass. Recently restored
to its original appearance – as recorded
in a watercolour of 1826 (fig. 118) – it is
encrusted with sculpture and has a
curiously shaped aperture in the floor.
An iron balustrade allows visitors to lean
over and peer into the gloomy Catacombs
below. The Ante Room was described by
Mrs Hofland as 'a small but fascinating
receptacle of precious things', which include
a cast of Michelangelo's *Taddei Tondo* and a
marble intarsia panel depicting a chariot
drawn by stags. All the contents of the
Ante Room survived in the museum and
were reinstated in their original positions
in 2015–16 (fig. 119).

Fig. 118
Joseph Michael Gandy
View of the Corridor next the Breakfast Room,
28 October 1826, watercolour, 336 × 196 mm
(13¼ × 7¾ in.)

This shows the Ante Room, a narrow lobby
crowded with sculpture and works of art, and
its unusual link with the Catacombs below.

Oct 28. 1826

View of the Corridor next the Breakfast Room.

Fig. 119
A plaster figure of Flora on the north wall of the
Ante Room, after the famous antique marble statue
once in the Palazzo Farnese, Rome, and now in the
Museo Archeologico Nazionale, Naples.

64

Visitors next enter the domed **Breakfast Room**. This is perhaps the most famous room in the museum, and justly so, for nowhere is Soane's mastery of volume and light better demonstrated than here (figs. 121–25). Built at the same time as the rest of the house in 1812, it is a sophisticated miniature version of one of the great top-lit banking halls Soane designed for the Bank of England, showing how the architect used his own house as a sort of laboratory for developing his architectural ideas. Over the breakfast table hovers one of Soane's favourite motifs, a shallow, canopy-like dome, springing directly from the piers and supported by four segmental arches studded with circular convex mirrors. In the centre is 'an octangular lantern-light, enriched with eight scriptural subjects in painted glass'. To the north and south, hidden skylights filter golden light into the ends of the room. Interestingly, the convex mirrors were an afterthought, added in the mid-1830s; the large mirrors in the corners of the dome were previously circular voids.

Fig. 120
One of two small portraits of Napoleon Bonaparte that hang on the south wall of the Breakfast Room. Said to have been painted by an Italian artist called Cossia in Verona in 1797, it shows the French ruler in his twenty-eighth year.

OPPOSITE
Fig. 121
The Breakfast Room in No. 13 Lincoln's Inn Fields. Its shallow 'handkerchief' dome is studded with dozens of convex mirrors, large and small.

Fig. 122
Detail of the octagonal lantern of the Breakfast
Room, set with panels of Flemish stained glass.

Fig. 123
The window embrasure of the Breakfast Room
opens up to reveal displays of small pictures, some
of them set within mirrored surrounds. Here an
engraved portrait of Giovanni Battista Belzoni faces
a drawing of an elaborate Antique ceiling, probably
by Agostino Brunias.

OPPOSITE
Fig. 124
The black marble chimneypiece displays a group of
sculptures by John Flaxman. Beyond, glazed internal
doors allowed Soane to keep an eye on his museum
from the comfort of his Breakfast Room.

Like most of the rooms in Lincoln's Inn Fields, the Breakfast Room is lined with bookcases; Soane had nearly 7000 books on his death and found it difficult to accommodate them all. As in the Library and Dining Room, extensive use is made of mirrors (there are more than a hundred in the room), over the chimneypiece, in strips set into the bookcases and even over the desk in the window. The canted panels flanking the window are hinged planes containing yet more works of art, surrounded by slips of mirror, while the glazed doors looking on to the Dome can be closed with additional mirrored leaves. The chimneypiece – with yet more tiny convex mirrors – was conceived as a sort of shrine to Soane's friend Flaxman, while over the bookcase is Gandy's watercolour of the Soane family tomb (see also fig. 24). Erected in St Pancras burial ground in 1815 after the death of Mrs Soane, and the resting place of Soane himself, it is perhaps his most influential building – its distinctive flattened dome was probably the inspiration for Sir Giles Gilbert Scott's (1880–1960) once ubiquitous K2 telephone box of 1924–26 (fig. 37). Scott was a Life Trustee of the museum between 1925 and 1960.

Climbing the **Staircase**, visitors ascend to the first floor of the house, passing on the half-landing the **Shakespeare Recess**. Restored in 2012, this diminutive marbled recess contains a plaster cast of the Bard's effigy from his tomb in Stratford-upon-Avon, stained glass and Shakespearean-themed paintings (figs. 126 and 127). The Soanes greatly admired Shakespeare, and it was Mrs Soane who bought the large picture of a scene from *The Merry Wives of Windsor* – *Falstaff in disguise led out by Mrs Page* by James Durno (*c.* 1745–1795) – that hangs on the stairs (see fig. 45).

Fig. 125
The north-west corner of the Breakfast Room. Even in Soane's day, books were stored all over the house.

Figs. 126 and 127
The Shakespeare Recess on the landing off the main Staircase. The bust of Shakespeare is a cast from the Bard's tomb in Stratford-upon-Avon.

The **North Drawing Room** is the first of the Soanes' reception rooms on the upper floor of the house. Looking out over the Monument Court towards a garniture composed of a colossal bust of Hercules flanked by ammonites (fig. 133), it is decorated en suite with the South Drawing Room, and was restored in 2013–14. The room is hung with architectural compositions by Gandy and a richly framed seapiece by Turner (fig. 128). Again, hinged planes maximize the number of works that can be hung, and Soane's arrangement of pictures over the chimneypiece on the east wall has been reinstated – dominated by *The Opening of London Bridge, August 1st 1831* by George Jones (1786–1869) in its rich, gilded composition frame (fig. 129). In the centre of the room stands the Dance Cabinet, a monumental plan chest containing the drawings of George Dance the Younger (fig. 130). Soane was trained in the Dance office and acquired the cabinet from Dance's son in 1836.

Fig. 128
Joseph Mallord William Turner
Admiral Van Tromp's Barge at the entrance to the Texel, 1645, 1831, oil on canvas, 900 × 1220 mm (35¼ × 48⅛ in.), framed

J.M.W. Turner was a personal friend of the Soanes and the architect's ally at the Royal Academy of Arts, where this picture was exhibited in 1831.

Fig. 129
Charles James Richardson
The North Drawing Room, 1835,
watercolour, 187 × 254 mm (7³⁄₈ × 10 in.)

This view shows the original hang of pictures in
the room, and the blue chintz cushions on the cane
seats of the mahogany chairs.

Fig. 130
The Dance Cabinet in the North Drawing Room.
This massive plan chest contains architectural
drawings by Soane's master, George Dance the
Younger. Acquired from Dance's son in 1836, it was
known as 'the shrine'.

The **South Drawing Room** was the Soanes' principal reception room, with three large windows commanding a fine view of Lincoln's Inn Fields (fig. 131). The glazed loggia beyond (fig. 132) was originally open to the elements and was brought into the room only in 1834 by Soane, who created within its narrow confines a clever perspective achieved with thin reeded colonnettes, busts and casts, and panels of stained glass. The sulphurous 'patent yellow' of the room is the Soanes' decorative scheme, reinstated to its original specification by Curator Peter Thornton in 1986–87, together with the matching yellow taffeta curtains with crimson trimmings and a busy Brussels carpet. The ceiling of the room, with its shallow 'domical compartments' and runs of 'bead moulding', is particularly refined, while the curved apsidal end wall disguises the irregular site of the house. The room is sparsely furnished, after the fashion of the day, and hung with family portraits – Soane and his sons, John and George, painted by William Owen, and a wistful pencil sketch of Mrs Soane by John Flaxman.

Fig. 131
The South Drawing Room, on the first floor of the house, was the principal room for entertaining, and Mrs Soane held musical recitals here. Note the ceiling 'formed of domical compartments and flat surfaces, encircled with a variety of architectural decorations'. The strong 'patent yellow' walls and matching upholstery were restored in 1986–87. Portraits by William Owen of Soane and his two sons hang on either side of the chimneypiece.

Fig. 132
Vista down the glazed loggia fronting Lincoln's Inn Fields, showing the bronzed reeded columns and a narrow window filled with grisaille stained-glass panels depicting saints, with violet borders.

Fig. 133
View into the Monument Court, showing sculpture on the roof at the back of the museum – a bust of Hercules, flanked by ammonites. The many skylights and lanterns require constant repair and refurbishment.

Fig. 134
Joseph Michael Gandy
View of the upper part of the Staircase, 1825,
watercolour, 220 × 151 mm (8¾ × 6 in.)

This view shows the landing, which formed the
entrance to Soane's Private Apartments and
featured a series of stained-glass windows.

Fig. 135
A small recess off the Staircase houses a display
of original models by the sculptors John Flaxman,
Sir Francis Chantrey and Thomas Banks.

OPPOSITE
Fig. 136
The Oratory. The little urn under a glass dome is
a Wedgwood 'blank', decorated by Mrs Soane with
dried flowers. Soane designed this space as a
memorial to his late wife.

Soane actually lived on the second floor of the house, and although his **Private Apartments** were turned into staff accommodation shortly after his death, the rooms were restored in 2013–15 as part of the 'Opening up the Soane' project, and are now shown to the public in special tours. En route you encounter the **Tivoli Recess**, a tiny sculpture gallery that stands off the half-landing (fig. 135). Restored in 2012, the recess contains plaster models by Soane's sculptor friends – John Flaxman, Sir Francis Chantrey and Thomas Banks – as well as a frieze from the Temple of Vesta in Tivoli and a large stained-glass window, *Charity*, by William Collins (1788–1847), after Sir Joshua Reynolds. The window was almost completely destroyed during World War II and had to be re-created especially, as did the unusual ceiling with its plaster sunburst and spandrels featuring eagles grasping writhing snakes.

On the second floor was Mrs Soane's Morning Room and her former bedroom, turned by Soane into the Model Room – a setting for his architectural models – in 1834. Soane's own Bedroom was also on this floor, being entered from a well-appointed Bathroom, while the Book Passage and a narrow space christened the Oratory completed the ensemble. Visitors catch glimpses of the **Oratory** (fig. 136) as they ascend the Staircase, through the internal windows set with antique panels of stained glass of Swiss, German and Flemish origin. Indeed, Soane formed an important collection of antiquarian stained glass, and nowhere is it more in evidence than in his Private Apartments. Inside, the Oratory is hung with prints and drawings, and contains an altar-like stand that was intended as a memorial to Soane's wife.

Mrs Soane's Morning Room (fig. 139) is entered via a curved corridor, behind which lurked an up-to-date water closet. Note the distinctive doors inset with convex mirrors. Soane kept the room as a shrine to his wife after her death in 1815, and the room is hung with family portraits and memorabilia.

The filigree ivory table is Indian and was
probably made in Murshidabad, Bengal,
in the late eighteenth century (fig. 138).
The story that the table – together with its
matching 'burgomeister' chairs – belonged
to Tipu Sultan and was looted from his
palace at Seringapatam is a romantic
legend, as is Sir John's proud claim that
the tortoiseshell casket was a gift from
Phillip II of Spain to Mary Tudor. Over
the chimneypiece hangs Clara Maria
Pope's (1768–1838) watercolour *Shakespeare's
Flowers* (fig. 137), a commission of about
1835, while towards the window is
J.M.W. Turner's *Kirkstall Abbey*, which Eliza
Soane purchased from the artist in 1804.
On the opposite wall hangs George Jones's
The Smoking House at Chelsea Hospital (1834)
– a reminder of Soane's role as Clerk of
Works to the Royal Hospital in Chelsea.

Mrs Soane's bedchamber occupied the
large room next door, but Soane converted
it in 1834 to display his collection of
architectural models. Long used as an
office, the **Model Room** (fig. 140) has
recently been reinstated – an ambitious
undertaking that included the restoration
of Soane's imposing Pompeiian model
stand (which incorporates a capacious plan
chest for architectural drawings) to its
original dimensions (fig. 141). The models –
more than one hundred of them survive at
the Soane Museum, constituting one of the
most important collections of historic
architectural models anywhere – include
a very large model of the excavations at
Pompeii as they were in 1820, purchased
by Soane from the sale of the collector-
architect John Sanders, Soane's first pupil,
in 1826. Made out of cork, it was probably
produced by Domenico Padiglione,
model-maker to the Royal Museum at
Naples, and cleverly imitates the eroded
stone of the ancient structures. Padiglione
probably also made the three cork models
of the Doric temples at Paestum, but the
model of the circular Temple of Vesta at
Tivoli, dated '177–', is signed by another
maker, Giovanni Altieri.

OPPOSITE
Fig. 137
A detail of the Morning Room, with Clara Maria Pope's *Shakespeare's Flowers*, a depiction of every flower mentioned in the Bard's plays.

ABOVE
Fig. 138
The restored Morning Room, with its reprinted hand-blocked wallpaper and idiosyncratic picture hang.

Fig. 139
Mrs Soane's Morning Room, engraving from *The Graphic*, 1 November 1884, 94 × 94 mm (3¾ × 3¾ in.)

Mrs Soane died in the winter of 1815, but for more than twenty years afterwards Soane maintained this room exactly as she had it. The ebony-and-tortoiseshell casket on the table is fancifully reputed to have belonged to Mary Tudor.

Another remarkable series of models is the twenty meticulously detailed white plaster models of restored ancient structures made by the Parisian model-maker François Fouquet (*fl.* 1810–20). Soane bought them from the sale of the architect Edward Cresy in 1834 for £100. Yet other models are Soane's own design and presentation models in painted wood and plaster, for structures that include the Bank of England; various government buildings erected in and around Whitehall; churches; and funerary monuments. They are shown exactly as Soane displayed them in the last decade of his life, while on the walls hang yet more ambitious architectural watercolours by Joseph Michael Gandy.

The recent restoration has put back the curious arrangements of mirrors that reflected the collection, while paintings and plaster casts have been returned to the little loggia overlooking Lincoln's Inn Fields. In the bookcases, the diminutive biscuit porcelain figures depicting medieval figures are part of a chess set designed by

Fig. 140
View in the Model Room, lithograph from Soane's 1835 *Description* ..., 275 × 380 mm (10⅞ × 15 in.), plate XXXVIII

From about 1834 Soane displayed his collection of architectural models in a large, south-facing room on the second floor of the house, which had once been Mrs Soane's bedchamber.

Fig. 141
The Pompeiian model stand was restored in 2013 from cut-down fragments, and now displays Soane's impressive collection of architectural models in wood, cork and plaster.

the celebrated sculptor John Flaxman. A glass case containing a collection of bronzes and small antiquities stands in front of the other window.

Off the Model Room is Soane's **Bathroom** (fig. 142), which acted as a sort of antechamber to his Bedroom. The bath has been restored using the original mahogany front, side and lid, which had been found reused elsewhere in the house (fig. 144). It was originally fully plumbed in, and this was the bath in which Soane sealed up a collection of papers and miscellaneous objects in November 1836, shortly before his death – a 'time capsule' that was reopened by the trustees of the museum only in November 1896. The array of blue-and-white porcelain – Oriental and English – on the fretwork hanging shelves over the chimneypiece is from Soane's collection (fig. 143). Large areas of the original red-and-ochre wallpaper survived around the chimneypiece, together with the red and black striped borders. These

provided the evidence that enabled the paper to be reproduced by Adelphi of New York, using handmade wooden blocks. This wallpaper is used throughout the Private Apartments, with a slightly different colourway in the Model Room and the Morning Room. A long-case clock by Threlkeld lurks in its own, specially designed, niche. Giving off the Bathroom, framed by a pair of metal reeded columns, is Soane's **Bedroom** (fig. 145), which has been carefully reconstructed from old inventory descriptions and bills. Among the items on show is his mahogany bed, with its 'fawn colour Super Moreen' hangings, 'bound with silk ornamental lace'.

Returning to the Model Room, visitors leave via the **Book Passage** (fig. 146), which features – as well as books – a glass-fronted box containing mummified cats that Soane discovered, walled up, in two of the old buildings he refurbished. High up in the ingenious sun-tube light well hangs Christopher Hünneman's portrait of a young Soane, aged twenty-two or twenty-three (fig. 4).

The restoration of Soane's Private Apartments was carried out in a project managed by Helen Dorey, Deputy Director and Inspectress of the Museum, in 2013–15, and was underpinned by a wealth of documentary, visual and physical evidence, as well as the survival of most of the former contents of the rooms. The project has enabled the museum to put on display hundreds of original artefacts from the collection – not only the pictures, sculpture, models and a profusion of stained glass, but also Soane's simple bedroom furniture and domestic bric-a-brac. Thus, the poignant story of the 'Soanes at home' can at last be told in the rooms that they reserved for their own occupation, an architect's private Elysium that has been lost to public view since the mid-nineteenth century.

OPPOSITE
Fig. 142
Charles James Richardson
View of the Bath Room, 1825, watercolour,
153 × 192 mm (6 × 7⅝ in.)

Fig. 143
The overmantel in the Bathroom differs from that shown in the watercolour of 1825. Just before his death, Soane rigged up this arrangement of hanging shelves to display his blue-and-white china.

Fig. 144
Soane's mahogany bath was carefully re-created from surviving fragments; the lid, front and side were found in the museum being used as panelling.

ABOVE
Fig. 145
Charles James Richardson
View of the Bed Room, 1825, watercolour,
178 × 237 mm (7 × 9⅜ in.)

Soane's Private Apartments on the second floor of No. 13 Lincoln's Inn Fields were surprisingly modest, although they were described as 'the very acmé of convenience, elegance and comfort' in his 1835 *Description* of the museum.

Visitors leave Sir John Soane's Museum via No. 12 Lincoln's Inn Fields, the Soanes' first house on the square. This was restored in 2011–12 to house improved facilities, including **Conservation Studios**, the **Soane Gallery** for temporary exhibitions, a **Shop**, a **Cloakroom** and a **Lift**. The opportunity was taken to research and reinstate the striking decorative schemes that the Soanes commissioned when they moved into the house in 1794: Pompeiian red in the front part of the gallery, relieved with fictive 'harewood' graining and a ceiling painted to resemble the sky; a greyish pink in the rear part of the gallery, with a coral and black striped border; and the **Staircase** painted to resemble sooty masonry. No attempt has been made to refurnish the house; Soane's furniture and collections are all displayed as he left them, in No. 13 Lincoln's Inn Fields. The only exception is the **Breakfast Room** (fig. 147), the rear ground-floor room, with its distinctive groined ceiling painted to imitate a creeper-hung trellis, which is recorded in a watercolour of 1798 by Joseph Michael Gandy (fig. 11). This was restored and refurnished with largely replica pieces in 1994–95, using funds provided by the Sir John Soane's Museum Foundation in the United States.

Fig. 146
The lantern of the Book Passage, seen from the glass doors in the attic. This unusual 'sun-tube' is hung with Soane designs and – Dorian Gray-like – his youthful portrait.

OPPOSITE
Fig. 147
The Breakfast Room, No. 12 Lincoln's Inn Fields. This, the only room in John and Eliza Soane's first house in Lincoln's Inn Fields to be shown furnished, was restored in 1994–95 on the basis of Joseph Michael Gandy's watercolour view of the room of 1798 (see fig. 11).

Present-day Floor Plans of the Museum

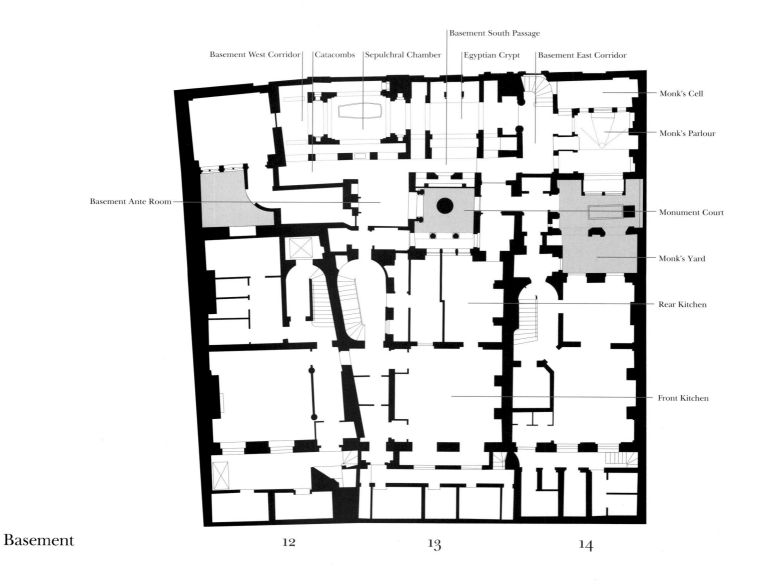

Basement West Corridor | Catacombs | Sepulchral Chamber | Basement South Passage | Egyptian Crypt | Basement East Corridor

Monk's Cell

Monk's Parlour

Basement Ante Room

Monument Court

Monk's Yard

Rear Kitchen

Front Kitchen

Basement

12   13   14

N

0   10   20   30   40   50 FEET

0   5   10   15 METRES

Foyle Space   Apollo Recess   Dome   Colonnade   Museum Corridor   Staircase to mezzanine Students' Room

Museum South Passage

Picture Room

Picture Room Recess

Dressing Room Recess

Ante Room

Dressing Room

Breakfast Room

Study

No. 12 Breakfast Room

Dining Room

Staircase

Inner Lobby

Shop

Library

Entrance Hall

Ground floor

12   13   14

153

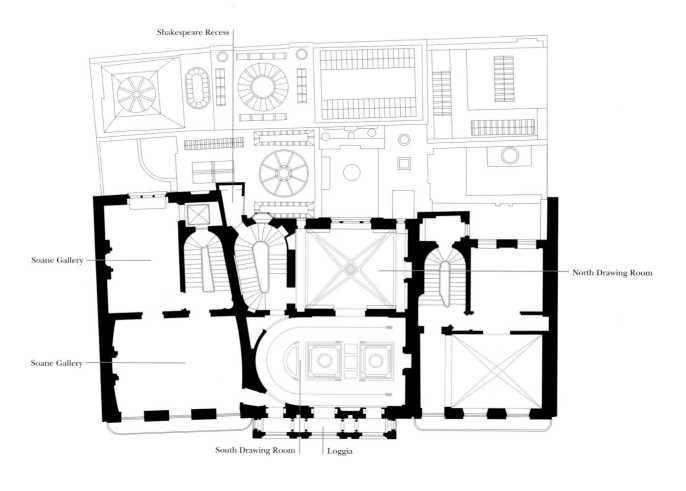

Shakespeare Recess

Soane Gallery

Soane Gallery

North Drawing Room

South Drawing Room   Loggia

First floor   12   13   14

N

0	10	20	30	40	50 FEET
0		5		10	15 METRES

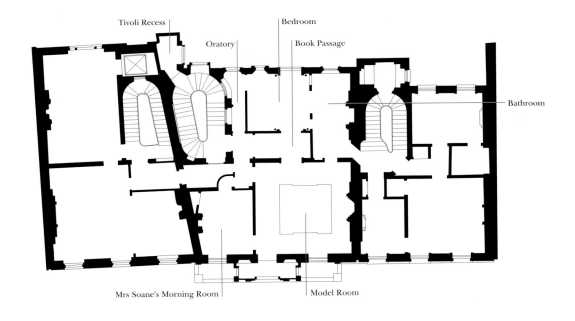

Tivoli Recess

Oratory

Bedroom

Book Passage

Bathroom

Mrs Soane's Morning Room

Model Room

Second floor   12   13   14

Further Reading

John Britton, *The Union of Architecture, Sculpture and Painting*, London 1827

Gillian Darley, *John Soane: An Accidental Romantic*, London and New Haven, Conn., 1999, 2nd edn 2000

Ptolemy Dean, *Sir John Soane and London*, Aldershot 2006

Helen Dorey (ed.), *Sir John Soane's Museum: A Complete Description*, London 2013

Hooked on Books: The Library of Sir John Soane, exhib. cat., ed. Eileen Harris and Nick Savage, Sir John Soane's Museum, London 2004

John Soane: Master of Space and Light, exhib. cat., ed. Margaret Richardson and MaryAnne Stevens, Royal Academy of Arts, London 2000

Susan Palmer, *At Home with the Soanes*, London 2015

John Soane, *Description of the Residence of John Soane, Architect*, London 1830, revised edns 1832 and 1835 (with remarks by Barbara Hofland)

Dorothy Stroud, *Sir John Soane, Architect*, London 1984, 2nd edn 1996

John Summerson, *Sir John Soane*, London 1952

Peter Thornton and Helen Dorey, *A Miscellany of Objects from Sir John Soane's Museum*, London 1992

Acknowledgements

Sir John Soane's Museum would like to acknowledge the generous help towards the costs of commissioning new photography from the museum's friends at Sir John Soane's Museum Foundation in the United States.

Elizabeth and Stanley D. Scott
Ike Kligerman & Barkley Architects
and
San Francisco Patrons' Circle members:
John A. Gunn and Cynthia Fry Gunn
Paul Vincent Wiseman/The Wiseman Group
F. Scott and Terry Gross
Kathleen and Fred Taylor/The Lotus Collection
Suzanne Tucker and Timothy F. Marks
Grant K. Gibson
Dorrit Egli
Valera Lyles
Richard L. Finch
Suzanna Schlemmer Allen

The author is grateful for the help of his colleagues at Sir John Soane's Museum, notably Xanthe Arvanitakis, Stephen Astley, Julie Brock, Helen Dorey, Susan Palmer and Kate Wilkinson. Also thanks to Selina Fellows, Todd Longstaffe-Gowan and Derry Moore, and to Julian Honer, Nicola Bailey and Lucy Smith of Merrell.

Index

JACKET FRONT: The Dome, with Sir Francis
  Chantrey's bust of Sir John Soane
  surrounded by cinerary urns and
  sculptural fragments.
JACKET BACK: Joseph Michael Gandy
  Detail from *Design for an extended elevation
  for 13–15 Lincoln's Inn Fields*, 1813,
  watercolour, showing Mr and Mrs Soane
  on the loggia balcony. The right-hand
  range, with the Ionic colonnade, was
  never realized.
PAGE 2: A convex mirror reflects the
  cantilevered Staircase. The simple reeded
  frame of the mirror is typical of Soane's
  discreet Neo-classical style.
PAGES 4–5: The Dome: statuettes of
  Michelangelo and Raphael by John
  Flaxman flank a giant marble lion's paw,
  which supports Chantrey's bust of Sir John
  Soane from 1828.
PAGE 7: A lively fragment of marble drapery
  in the Dome area.
PAGES 10–11: Joseph Michael Gandy
  Detail from *The Plan and Interior of the
  Ground Floor of a Town House*, 1822,

watercolour. This shows the principal
  interiors of No. 13 Lincoln's Inn Fields
  (see fig. 23).
PAGE 46: The *Pasticcio*, a towering confection
  symbolizing the progress of architecture,
  in the Monument Court. It incorporates a
  distinctive Corinthian capital from the
  Bank of England, possibly a reject from
  the mason's yard. Soane was an inveterate
  collector of architectural salvage (see
  fig. 57).
PAGE 157: An Ionic capital perches on a shelf
  in the Colonnade.
PAGE 160: Detail of Sir Francis Chantrey's
  marble bust of Sir John Soane (1828; see
  fig. 32).

Published by Merrell Publishers, London
and New York

Merrell Publishers Limited
70 Cowcross Street
London EC1M 6EJ

merrellpublishers.com

First published 2009; revised edition 2013;
revised and updated 3rd edition 2016

Text copyright © 2009, 2013 and 2016
  Sir John Soane's Museum, London
Illustrations copyright © 2009, 2013 and 2016
  Sir John Soane's Museum, London, with
  the exception of those listed on page 156
Design and layout copyright © 2009, 2013
  and 2016 Merrell Publishers Limited

British Library Cataloguing in Publication
Data. A catalogue record for this book is
available from the British Library.

ISBN 978-1-8589-4649-8

Produced by Merrell Publishers Limited
Designed by Dennis Bailey
Plans drawn by Christopher H. Woodward
Copy-edited by Elisabeth Ingles
Proof-read by Linda Schofield
Indexed by Hilary Bird

Printed and bound in China